Once the Acacias Bloomed

Memories of a Childhood Lost

Fred Spiegel

Edited by Maryann McLoughlin O'Donnell, Ph.D.
A project of the Holocaust Resource Center
The Richard Stockton College of New Jersey

COMTEQ
PUBLISHING
MARGATE, NEW JERSEY

Published by:
    ComteQ Publishing
    A division of ComteQ Communications, LLC
    P.O. Box 3046
    Margate, New Jersey 08402
    609-487-9000 • Fax 609-822-4098
    Email: publisher@ComteQcom.com
    Website: www.ComteQpublishing.com

ISBN 0-9674074-6-X
Library of Congress Control Number: 2004108263

Book design by Rob Huberman
Cover design by Jacob Pezzicola

Printed in the United States of America
10 9 8 7

Praise for *Once the Acacias Bloomed*

"Spiegel, a child survivor of three camps, has written a compelling and accessible memoir which, in his words, is an effort 'to reach across the barriers of understanding.' In this, he succeeds admirably, offering the reader not only his chilling story but also his postwar reflections on causes of the Shoah, and on contemporary Germany. Most importantly, Mr. Spiegel succinctly addresses the issues of bigotry, antisemitism and terrorism, and our ethical obligation to speak out against racial hatred. A must read!"

Elizabeth R. Baer
Ida E. King Distinguished Visiting Professor of Holocaust Studies for 2004
Richard Stockton College of New Jersey

"This memoir will be an important contribution to the study of the Holocaust. Each of these episodes will assist students in learning about the Holocaust and its effect on children. The New Jersey Commission on Holocaust Education endorses the reading of this memoir by middle and high school students."

Paul B. Winkler, Executive Director
The New Jersey Commission On Holocaust Education

"*Once the Acacias Bloomed* is an extraordinary book, more than 'simply' the memoir of a child survivor of the Holocaust who wants to record his experiences. It is a book of wonderful insight, quiet dignity, and great humanity. When you read his book, you will see that Fred Spiegel did more than survive the Holocaust. He triumphed over the inhumanity of the Nazis by overcoming his lost childhood, creating his own humanity, embracing love, bringing new life into this world, and holding on to hope for a better world. *Once the Acacias Bloomed* is a book to be read, savored, and shared. I wholeheartedly recommend it."

Dr. Carol Rittner, R.S.M.
Distinguished Professor of Holocaust & Genocide Studies
The Richard Stockton College of New Jersey

"The clarity and conciseness of the author in describing the most painful and moving moments of his life can be seen in all the details of this extraordinary book that the reader will have difficulty putting aside."

Gottfried Wagner
Author of Twilight of the Wagners – the Unveiling of a family's Legacy *and scholar of German-Jewish history and the Shoah.*

"Every survivor memoir is as unique as the multitude of individual experiences during the Holocaust. Fred Spiegel is able to combine surprisingly detailed and vivid recollections from his 'lost' childhood with the background and context learned after the fact. By clearly distinguishing between the two, Spiegel does a great service to his readers. I recommend this book to high school students, college students, and researchers alike."

Michael Hayse, Associate Professor of History
Richard Stockton College of New Jersey

Dedication

This book is dedicated to the memory of the members of my family murdered in the *Shoah* – the Holocaust.

To my Uncle Max Spiegel, Aunt Paula, and their son, my cousin Alfred. They tried so hard to make us feel at home while we lived in Dinxperlo.

To my Uncle Hertog Weijel, my Aunt Margarete (Grete) and their young son, Abraham (Brammie), just five years old when he was murdered. I have very fond memories of them, especially the vacation I spent with them in the summer of 1942.

To the six million Jews who perished in the Holocaust, and especially the nearly one and a half million innocent children.

To my cousin Ruth Spiegel, who was the daughter of Uncle Max. Ruth was the only survivor in her family, having survived Vught, Auschwitz, and Ravensbrück, only to suffer for the rest of her life; her body survived but her spirit did not.

To my Grandfather Louis Spiegel, who tried to take care of me when I was a little boy, but did not understand what was happening to his beloved Fatherland.

And to my Grandfather Julius Berghausen and his wife Sophie, who were uprooted in their old age, but were always cheerful in my presence.

To my Uncle Adolf Spiegel, Aunt Martha, cousin Margot, and also cousin Alice, who died so young. After liberation, they again found me and my sister Edith and tried hard to make me feel at home after leaving Germany.

And, of course, to my mother, Elise Spiegel, who suffered so terribly while living in England during the war, not knowing what had happened to us.

Ani Ma'amin (I believe)
I believe
With Perfect Faith
In the coming of the Messiah.
And even though he tarry,
Still will I believe.

At the rising of the sun and at its going down,
We remember them.
At the blowing of the wind and in the chill of winter,
We remember them.
At the opening of the buds and the rebirth of spring,
We remember them.
At the shining of the sun and in the warmth of summer,
We remember them.
At the rustling of the leaves and in the beauty of autumn,
We remember them.
At the beginning of the year and at its end,
We remember them
As long as we live, they too will live;
For they are now part of us,
As we remember them
— Rabbi Sylvan Kamens

Exalted, compassionate God, grant perfect peace in Your
sheltering Presence, among the holy and the pure, to the souls of all
our brothers and sisters, men, women and children of the House of
Israel, who were slaughtered and buried, burnt and strangled
sanctifying God's Name. May their memory endure, inspiring truth
and loyalty in our lives. May their souls thus be bound up in the bond
of life. May they rest in peace. And let us say: Amen.

If the dead Jews would arise . . . .

If the dead Jews would arise and they would just give their names and whence they came, two years would go by. If all the Jews also announced how they were murdered—shot, beaten, strangled, gassed, burned—four years would go by. And if they went through roll call as in the camps, counting one by one, another year would go by.

--Karl Fruchtmann (translated from the German)

Table of Contents

Acknowledgements

I have been happily married for 34 years to my wonderful wife, Yael. We have three beautiful children: Omri, the oldest, born in 1972, who married his longtime girlfriend Nancy Gay on November 9, 2002. He graduated from York College in Pennsylvania and lives in Howell, New Jersey, a policeman who takes great pride in his job. Yuval, our middle son, born in 1975, is autistic and now lives in a group home of the agency New Horizons for Autism with other autistic adults. They have 24-hour supervision and a special work program. He is very content there. Our youngest child is our daughter, Avital. She was born in 1979, graduating from The Richard Stockton College of New Jersey. She lives in Northfield, in South New Jersey, and is a caseworker for ARC, The Association for Retarded Citizens. She plans to continue her studies for her Masters.

I am amazed at my wife, the way she has coped with Yuval, especially during the years he lived at home and went to the various special schools. He is a very loving child and will always remain a child. Yael and both my other children have always been very patient with Yuval and given him lots of love. I am very proud of their achievements.

My children know of my past, my childhood. However, I never spoke to them much about it, until 1989, our first trip to Holland and Germany. Ever since then they have been very interested in the subject of the Holocaust.

I owe a lot of thanks to my wife and children. Through their support and encouragement I was able to write this book, which was at times very difficult because of the terrible memories. I wrote this book mainly for them, for my sister Edith who lives in Chile, who was with me and who helped me to survive these horrors, and for my sister's family, and all my Chilean cousins and their families and future generations. I believe we have to forgive, but never forget.

Foreword

Triumph of the Spirit

If you have ever seen the national frenzy when the Dutch soccer team is doing well in the World Cup or when Dutch speed skaters reign at the Olympics, you would put some serious questions marks around the notion that the Dutch are a sober people. To borrow from Paul Simon, "...still crazy after all these years" seems to be a better description.

It is an irony that Fred Spiegel's recollections are so firmly embedded in that original concept of those sober and modest Dutch. He was not born in the Netherlands but in Germany. He only spent a few years in the Netherlands in freedom before his imprisonment as a Jew and before his deportation to Germany—now part of that horrible torrent known as the Holocaust, the vast landscape of the destruction of European Jewry.

In the most popular memoirs of those who survived, we are confronted with a universe of almost unbelievable horror (and we know that some American officials did not, could not believe, the early reports that a genocide of extraordinary scope was underway). Their memoirs also focus very much on the "auto" part of autobiography, on the anguish and the pain of the inner self in dealing with the incomprehensible fate that has come its way. They are mirrors of the soul, dealing with sheer survival, every hour, every day.

Fred Spiegel's recollections are, in essence, quite different. When the war surrounded him, he was a child and, on occasion, he tells us about his fright—it will chill your bones. But, more often than not, Fred's recollections are a reportage on what is happening not *in* him, not in his heart and soul, but *around* him. For someone to be so free of self-absorption is remarkable; for the memories of an interrupted childhood it is astonishing, and I believe rather unique—though Helen Colijn's *Song of Survival* (and the movie *Paradise Road* based on her experiences in a Japanese concentration camp) comes close. The beauty of Fred's recollection is in the power of his straight, unadorned eyewitness reporting.

Those among us who regularly deal with Holocaust survivors—psychologists, social workers, or scholars—cannot help but develop a deep and abiding empathy toward them: many are scarred by life-long trauma, anguish, and pain. For many, dealing with the shadows of history is a daily battle with a sledgehammer.

Fred is not free of such assaults. But Fred's eye witnessing is different. After you read this book, you do not feel hopeless. He is not a prisoner of hatred against those who planned and engineered the Holocaust against him and his people, as understandable as such hatred would be. He has no bias against *the* Germans—in fact he rarely uses that *the*. He bears no ill will against post-war German generations: the chapters in which he writes about his friendships with high school students in his native town who are studying his story are among the most moving in the memoir.

"From Despair, Hope" is the motto at my college's Holocaust Resource Center. Fred's life after the war exemplifies that hope and that is why his work—and this book—is so successful.

Perhaps the most powerful Nazi propaganda movie was *Triumph of the Will*. Instead of that, you have in your hands a *Triumph of the Spirit*. It is an extraordinary tale of one man's indomitable drive to live, and to live in grace despite what happened to him. May it inspire you, as does Fred's presence among those privileged to be his friends.

G. Jan Colijn, Ph.D., Dean of General Studies
The Richard Stockton College of New Jersey

Author's Preface

The soul shrinks
From all that it is about to remember.
    —Love Calls Me to the Things of the World," Richard Wilbur

At the going down of the sun and in the morning
We will remember them.
                —"For the Fallen," Laurence Binyon

I wrote this book so that future generations may know of the terrible events that happened during those years we now call the Holocaust, 1933-1945. It was not an easy task to write these stories, some of which are from my memories when I was just a child witnessing these events. When it was over in May of 1945, I was just thirteen years old. But, however painful, it is very important for survivors to bear witness in order to teach children what can happen when bigotry, racism, and antisemitism become the law of the land. I do believe we have to forgive; however, we must never forget or it may happen again. Future generations must understand what happened and why it happened. So, "however inadequate words are, human language is all we have to reach across the barriers of understanding."[1] This memoir is my attempt to reach across those barriers.

I had written a few articles over the years about my childhood experiences during the Holocaust, those terrible years, for me, from 1938–1945, for the local Jewish newspaper in Ocean County, New Jersey. But this was just the tip of the proverbial iceberg. Just a few memories and once the paper folded I stopped. After doing an interview on tape with Steven Spielberg's Foundation of the Survivors of the Shoah and viewing the results, a three and a half hour affair, I came to the conclusion that writing about my experiences would be even better because this would enable me to correct mistakes and omissions. I had also done two shorter interviews on tape, one for the Ocean County, New Jersey, Jewish Federation, with Anise Singer, and one for the Center for Holocaust Studies at Brookdale Community College in Lincroft, New Jersey, with Professor Seymour Siegler. I do think that all the interviews on tape are important documents but I felt it was not enough. I had joined the speakers' bureau at the Center and I started to go to local schools to lecture and speak about my experiences. This gave me the confidence to start writing more seriously.

In October 1999, I went to the Second International Conference on Holocaust and Education in the 21st century at Yad Vashem in Jerusalem, Israel, together with Professors Michael Hayse, Leo Lieberman, Carol Rittner, RSM, Gail Rosenthal of the Richard Stockton College of New Jersey, and then President of the College Dr. Vera King Farris. There were many workshops at this conference and one of them was called "Leave a Legacy Writing," conducted by Professor Ellen Gerstle of Fairleigh Dickenson and Drew Universities. This workshop was aimed at survivors, and I participated. After our return from Israel, Professor Gerstle invited me to participate in the "Leave-a-Legacy Writing Workshop for Survivors," which was being organized under the auspices of the Drew University Center for Holocaust/Genocide studies. We met for the first time in late fall of 1999, about twenty survivors and three professors of English Literature and we continued to meet off and on for three years. Each session was usually for three hours. We had a chance to write something while we were there and also were given "homework" to write about a specific experience. Most of us would then read what we had written for everybody to hear and also sometimes to critique.

Through this experience and the help, knowledge, leadership, and especially patience of Professors Jacqueline

Berke, Robert Ready and of course Ellen Gerstle, we learned a lot, and I learned what writing was all about. Drew University Center for Holocaust/Genocide studies is still planning to publish an anthology of some of our writings. They will probably publish about two or three of my stories. One of my stories, "*Yom Kippur* Eve 1942," was published in their publication *Perspectives on the Holocaust* and most likely will be one of the stories chosen for the anthology.

I was often asked, for example by the professors, "What were your feelings and emotions during those years? Try to put some of those emotions into your writing." This is very difficult because I was a child, trying to survive, so it is not easy to remember reactions and emotions. In addition, this all happened a long time ago. Almost sixty years have passed since liberation. For us, the child survivors, it was a lost childhood. These are my feelings and emotions today. During the war years and particularly when I was in the various camps I was hungry and frightened, especially those last few months in Bergen-Belsen when I was starving. After it was over, it was difficult to adjust and I could not return to being a child. It took me many years before I could settle down and lead a normal life. I believe that is the result of the trauma of my childhood.

The director of the Richard Stockton College Holocaust Resource Center, Gail Rosenthal, persuaded me that I should try to publish all my stories in book form. Jan Colijn, Michael Hayse, Gail Rosenthal, of Stockton College, and Mary Johnson of Facing History have read my story and suggested additions and revisions. Maryann McLoughlin has had the patience to edit my writing, and Dean Jan Colijn encouraged me throughout the process. I am grateful to them all. What follows is what I remember of those terrible years.

Fred Spiegel
February 2004

Editor's Preface

I have been working with Fred Spiegel on his book for over a year now. I have enjoyed working with Fred because he writes well and is congenial.

More importantly, his stories have both moved and enlightened me. As I was editing his book I asked myself, What group of students would most benefit from reading his memoir? My answer: I think the memoir is especially valuable—ethically and academically—for students from the seventh grades through college.

On an ethical level students can see the ethical choices that confronted many whom Fred tells about; these will remind them of the choices people have to make during crisis times but also about the kinds of choices they have to make even now about prejudice and racism.

On an academic level students will learn about the Holocaust and World War II from the perspective of a young boy, who was six years old during *Kristallnacht*, and who, when he was only seven years old, was separated from his mother for six years. They will read about Fred's courage and strength but also about the courage and strength of the people who helped Fred and his sister Edith to survive. But I think students will be especially impacted by Fred's courage and strength. After all, during this terrible epoch in our world's history, he is a child like them.

In order to make the book more available to students of all ages, we have divided the text into a number of sections: first, the Introductory material; second, the crux of Fred's story during the years 1938-45; and lastly, his reflection and commemoration of the Holocaust and an Afterword by Dan Bar-on. We have provided maps and a chronology to help students understand the place of Fred's story historically as well as geographically. In addition there is a Teacher's Guide available.

Maryann McLoughlin, Ph.D.
Richard Stockton College of New Jersey
Holocaust Resource Center

Once the Acacias Bloomed

PART I

Germany, 1932 -1938

....And overnight our thoughts grew gray. The sun
Sowed poison salt in open wounds. We choke.
White doves turned into owls. They're poking fun,
Mocking our dreams that disappeared in smoke.
—"Faces in Swamps," Abraham Sutzkever

The Park

It has begun, the tearing, the trampling on silks.
—"A Poor Christian Looks at the Ghetto," Czeslaw Milosz

Once I lived in a small town in Germany called Dinslaken at Bismarckstrasse 61. Dinslaken was a small town at that time, about 20,000 inhabitants. I was born there on April 21, 1932, to a German Jewish family. My family had been living in this general area for hundreds of years. My father, Sigmund Spiegel, loved to play *Fussball* (soccer) and I have a picture of him together with his teammates on the 1913 Dinslaken soccer team. He had been a sergeant in the German army in World War I and was badly wounded in the battle of Verdun. He had received many decorations for valor in battle, including the Iron Cross. My uncles and grandfather had also served in the German army. My father died in December 1933, when I was one year old, so I do not really remember him except from stories my mother and other people told me.

After my father's death, my grandfather, Louis Spiegel, came to live with us.[2] One of my earliest memories is of my grandfather playing *skat*, a German card game, in the evenings at our house with his friends and neighbors. My grandfather was well known and friends with nearly everybody in town. Behind our house there was a nice park and grandfather used to take me there for walks and to play with the neighborhood children. He would sit on one of the park benches and talk to his friends, while keeping a watchful eye on me.

Around 1936, when I was four or five years old things started to change and my park was not so nice anymore. Older kids started to pick on me, tried to beat me up, threw stones and dirt on me, and called me "dirty Jew." Then my grandfather's friends also started to curse him and he decided it was time to get out of the park. When I went home I asked my mother, "How come those kids call me 'dirty Jew'? Am I dirty? I took a bath this morning." After a few more incidents, we did not go to the park anymore, even though it was almost our back yard.

After that my grandfather started to take me to the Jewish Orphanage to play. The orphanage had been established many years earlier for the whole area called the Rhineland. It was much safer there in the huge house with the large fenced in yard. The older kids kept an eye on me while I played with the other little kids in the orphanage. It was really fun and I soon knew a lot of the kids. However, I longed to play in the park, the beautiful park by our backyard, with its big lawns, lake, and tall trees. But this had become too dangerous for a Jewish child. I never played there again.

Kristallnacht

I stood before the burning synagogue and watched as the fireman protected the surrounding buildings, being careful not to put any water on the isolated curls of smoke rising here and there from the devastated sanctuary that was once our synagogue.

I stood before the burning synagogue, unbelievingly, in deep shock, empty of strength, gutted, as was our synagogue. A murder had been committed, symbolic as it were, soon to be followed by the near annihilation of our people.

Slowly my senses returned in a wave of anger. I clenched my fists, my eyes filled with tears of outrage. My silence screamed: "Kooma Adonai, veyafootsoo oyvecha . . . ." "Rise up, Lord, and scatter your enemies."

But the clouds did not part, the shofar* did not sound, the strong hand and the outstretched arm did not appear.

It was not the year of the Lord. He had averted His face.

—"*Kristallnacht,*" Arnold Blum

November 9, 1938. That day and the next few days I will never forget for the rest of my life. I was six and a half years old, still living in Dinslaken. I was living with my mother, my older sister Edith, and my grandfather.

I had started going to school a few months before. As Jews were not allowed to go to the local schools anymore, we went to the Jewish school, which had been established many years earlier.[3] I remember Mr. Weinberg, the teacher, because he rented a room in our house. There was just this one teacher, plus a few teacher's aides.

**shofar:* a ram's horn trumpet blown during *Rosh Hashanah* (Jewish New Year) and at the conclusion of *Yom Kippur* (Day of Atonement).

My Aunt Klara was visiting us that day, November 9. It became dark early, and that evening I went to visit the elderly couple, Mr. and Mrs. Brockhausen, who rented a third floor apartment from my mother in our house. I had become very friendly with them and even though non-Jews were not supposed to rent from Jews any more, they had refused to leave. They invited me to come next morning and join them for breakfast, something I had often done in the past.

I woke up early the next morning, November 10. Looking out the window, I noticed a lot of smoke coming from the direction of the synagogue. Also groups of men were running around armed with pick axes and all sorts of other tools. I had no idea what they were doing and what was happening but it looked scary and threatening. I asked my mother, but she also did not know what was going on. Then I decided to go upstairs; maybe they knew something. After all Mr. Brockhausen was a retired policeman, surely he would know. When I arrived upstairs they were up and waiting for me. They did not know what was happening; at least that was what they said. However, when I asked them about the smoke, they said the synagogue was on fire, but the fire engines were there: "Not to worry, Fritz. The fire will surely be put out soon."

Mrs. Brockhausen was preparing the breakfast, when suddenly I heard a deafening noise downstairs coming from the direction of our apartment. Then I heard somebody smashing down the door and the noise of breaking glass. My mother and sister started to scream. I wanted to run downstairs, but Mr. Brockhausen held me back. I could clearly hear things being smashed downstairs and being thrown out of the window on to the street below. Finally I went downstairs. The entrance door to our apartment, which was partly glass, had been smashed. Upon entering I found that many things had been totally destroyed, the windows broken, and much of our furniture and crystal was on the pavement below. My mother, sister, and Aunt Klara were standing on the balcony crying. My grandfather had been arrested and taken away by two policemen. Mr. Brockhausen came in and tried to calm everybody. Soon the two policemen returned. We were told we could not stay in our apartment and had to go with them. On the way out, we passed by the downstairs apartment that was empty because the Abosch family, a Jewish family who had rented it from my mother, had been expelled to Poland a few weeks earlier. Their apartment was totally destroyed.[4]

People were standing in the street and watching as the Jewish families left their houses and some of them spit at us and threw stones and sand. We passed by the synagogue—still burning. The policemen brought us to the Jewish school, where we were told that we had to stay overnight. Apparently after we left our apartment, some of the Nazis came back. They tried to set the house on fire. Mr. Brockhausen stopped them, claiming the house belonged to him.

In the middle of the night my mother woke me up. She wanted me to say goodbye to my babysitter from the orphanage, Francisca Grabownik. As I found out years later, the children still living in the orphanage were terribly abused during *Kristallnacht*. The Jewish community had then decided to take the thirty children from the orphanage to Cologne (Köln), Germany, from where they were sent afterwards to Belgium and Holland to try to keep them out of harm's way. That night was the last time I ever saw Francisca. Most of the about 30 children living in the Orphanage at the time of *Kristallnacht* did not survive the Holocaust. According to the diary kept by Yitzhak Sophoni Herz, director of the orphanage at that time:

The police ordered us to get ready for a march through the Center of Dinslaken. I was to be responsible for preparing this march. The news that there would be a Judenparade *(a parade of Jews) through town spread like wildfire. The people of Dinslaken stood three and four deep along the sidewalk to await the* Judenparade. *Most people cursed and taunted us but on the faces of a few there was disgust at the proceedings. In front of the parade were two policemen, flanked by uniformed Nazis. The little children of the orphanage were forced to climb into a hay wagon and four older boys were forced to pull this wagon.*

The Jewish cemetery, where my father and grandmother were buried, was not spared either. It was completely vandalized; headstones were smashed and overturned. A few days after *Kristallnacht* we left our house in Dinslaken. My mother sent Edith and me to live with relatives in Holland. The border into Holland had been closed for refugees leaving Germany; however, after the *Kristallnacht* pogrom the Dutch authorities relented and allowed children who had relatives living in Holland to come into their country.

PART II

The Netherlands, 1938-43

Where the broad ocean leans against the land.
—"The Traveller," Oliver Goldsmith

I have been a stranger in a strange land.
—Exodus, 2:22

Uncle Adolf

*How mighty the price survival commands
A childhood forever denied.*
—"A Childhood Denied," Dunio Bernharut

In November 1938, a few days after Kristallnacht, Edith and I went to our relatives in Gennep, Holland. We had many close relatives living in Holland. Uncle Adolf, my father's older brother, and his family lived in Gennep, in the southern province of Limburg, near the river Maas. Uncle Max, another brother of my father's, lived with his family in Dinxperlo. Both families had left Germany sometime after the Nazis came to power. Also my newly married Aunt Margarete lived in Enschede with her Dutch husband, Hertog Weijel. As a little boy I had visited all of them and knew them well, so it was really no shock for me when my mother decided to send my sister Edith and me to Gennep after *Kristallnacht* to live with Uncle Adolf, Aunt Martha, and my cousins—Margot, about twelve years, and Alice, ten.

We started school in Gennep almost immediately after the Christmas vacation in the beginning of January 1939. I was almost seven years old and of course did not know any Dutch but I learned very quickly. We went to a one-room schoolhouse, a very large room, so I could always see my sister and my cousins who sat with their classes in a different part of the room. I remember best my cousin Alice, one of the brightest pupils in school. She was almost three years older than I, a very kind and considerate child who took a special interest in me and tried to help with my lessons and especially to teach me Dutch. She was very popular, liked by everyone. However, she was sick quite often; nobody seemed to know what was wrong with her. The head mistress of the school, Mrs. Verbiest, came to our house frequently to visit, especially if Alice had been absent and also to tell my aunt about my progress.

I was quite happy in Gennep; I liked living with my uncle, aunt, and cousins, who were all very good to me. I made a lot of new friends and soon spoke Dutch reasonably well.

Some of my friends were from the gypsy camp on the outskirts of town. I became very friendly with two of the kids, a brother and sister. I used to go and play there after school and they were always very nice and kind to me. But my aunt did not like the idea of my going to the gypsy camp; when I came home she always said, "You'll catch fleas, if you stay there too long." I did continue to go there off and on, until one day the girl told me that they were leaving the area. I went back the next day but they were gone. Nobody seemed to know where they had gone, and nobody cared. I imagine my aunt was probably happy that I no longer could go to the gypsy camp to play.

I then became very friendly with a girl living in the neighborhood. Her parents, together with an uncle, owned a restaurant. They were very religious Catholics and they had a big cross and lots of icons in the corridor leading to the restaurant. Sometimes the girl would kneel in front of the cross, pray, and try to persuade me to do the same thing. I refused, so she said I was a *Hollandse Kaaskop*, a Dutch cheese head, which meant that I was a stubborn Dutch. I was very pleased when she said that, it made me feel pretty good after being less than one year in Holland.

Gennep was one of the few towns or villages in Holland where there was no synagogue or Jewish community. There were some Jewish families in town, most refugees from Germany. During the High Holidays in the fall of 1939 we did meet in somebody's house for prayer and to socialize.

Sometime in late 1939 two uncles, Isidore and Meier Hes, came to live with us for a short while. Isidore and Meier were cousins from Papenburg, Germany. Isidore, the husband of Klara Hes Spiegel, a sister of my father, had three children, my cousins: Josef, Louis and Julius. Meier Hes was married to Johanna Hes Spiegel, also a sister of my father.

Both families had managed to obtain visas to immigrate to Chile. The husbands came away from Germany to Gennep to stay with Uncle Adolf and Aunt Martha for a short while, in order to be out of "harm's way," while their families prepared to travel to Genoa, Italy. Isidore and Meier were supposed to rejoin their families once they arrived in Italy, in time to board their ship to South America.

A few weeks after their arrival, the local Dutch police knocked on the door. They had come to arrest Isidore, Meier, and Adolf. Apparently, Isidore and Meier had crossed the border illegally, as many German refugees had done. But why did they arrest Uncle Adolf? I never quite knew why. Apparently he had helped the cousins to cross the border and bring some money with them, as he had helped other refugees. Adolf had been in Gennep since 1936, helping Jews escape Germany and was involved in money exchanges with them. However, the Germans did not want the Jews to leave with any German money, so the Germans considered this illegal. Therefore, the German authorities had pressured the Dutch to arrest Uncle Adolf. Locally some other people wanted to see him in prison. So when they were picked up, quite a large crowd gathered and cheered when they departed in police custody. Was it because they were Germans? Or Jews? I never knew for sure. The three were put in prison in a nearby town, Roermond. After a few days Uncle Adolf was released, coming quietly back home. A little later, the Hes cousins were released, but they did not come back to Gennep, traveling straight on to meet their families in Italy. They made it to Chile with their families a few months later. I did not see them again until many years after the war.

CHAPTER FOUR: GENNEP

September 1, 1939

The unsheathing of the great knife of parting.
—"A Dead Child Speaks," Nelly Sachs

After *Kristallnacht*, November 9 and 10, 1938, my mother tried desperately to obtain visas for us to leave Europe. (She was not as lucky as Isidore and Meier Hes whose families had visas for Chile.) Nothing was available. The United States had closed its borders to immigration, especially Jewish immigration. Palestine, which today is Israel, was a British Mandate (territory administered by the British). The British Government had issued a "White Paper," an official Government document stopping any further Jewish immigration into Palestine. However, in August of 1939, my mother obtained a visa as an *au pair,* a foreign maid, for England. Unfortunately this visa did not allow her to take us with her.

During the First World War Holland had been neutral, a policy it would presumably pursue in the event of another war in Europe. So my mother thought we would be safe staying in

Holland for the time being, until she could make arrangements for us to join her in England.

On the way to England she decided to visit us for one week in Gennep. She was due to arrive on September 1, 1939. I was seven years old and had not seen my mother since November 1938, so I was tremendously excited, looking forward to seeing her again. I had such a lot to tell her. When my mother arrived, I ran into her arms and cried. Then my uncle came, gently pulling me away. He urgently needed to speak to her, for he had just heard the news on the radio that the German army had invaded Poland. He tried to explain to my mother that it would be better to leave immediately, as otherwise he feared that there would be no more passenger ships to England. He believed that Europe was going to be at war after the British and French ultimatum expired on September 3, 1939.

I was very disappointed and upset when my mother told me she had to leave within one hour. How could I tell her everything that had happened to me since I left home, about my new friends and school, and about Gennep—in one hour? After too short a time I said goodbye to her again. Little did I know at the time not only that I would not see her for more than six years but also what would happen to us and the terrible times that lay ahead. I am sure she could never have imagined the terror we would experience before we would be reunited. My mother did manage to take the very last passenger ship from Hoek van Holland to England on September 1, 1939.[5] As she left she promised that as soon as she was settled we would be reunited with her in England.

The German Invasion

Over the radio
I hear victory bulletins of the scum of the earth. Curiously
I examine a map of the continent. High up in Lapland
Towards the Arctic Ocean
I can still see a small door.
—Bertolt Brecht

May 10, 1940 was a day of infamy in Holland. The German army invaded without provocation or reason because Holland had declared its neutrality in the event of a war in Europe. The official start of the war on September 3, 1939, had not affected us in Gennep. However, some trenches were dug around the school and we had air raid drills in case of an attack.

The dawn of May 10 brought a beautiful, bright sunny morning, a typical Dutch spring morning. The day before I had done all my homework for school and had spent the evening playing with friends. But then I had woken up at night and heard some noise like airplanes in the sky. I did not pay much attention to this, almost immediately going back to sleep. The rays of the sun woke me up. I heard some strange and loud noises coming from the sky and also the street below. The sky was full of airplanes and some of them were flying quite low. I could see the German markings, including the swastika.

I looked down from my second floor bedroom to the cobblestone street running through the little town. German soldiers in full battle dress, helmets, rifles, and gas masks stood there with several tanks and trucks. Downstairs I heard my aunt speaking German and I heard a male voice answering, but it did not sound like my uncle. I dressed very quickly and went downstairs. My sister and cousins were in the living room, looking out the window at the German army. I went to the kitchen and saw my aunt talking to a German soldier who was sitting at the kitchen table waiting for her to brew him some coffee. My uncle, however, was nowhere to be seen. Apparently this German soldier had knocked on our door early in the morning and asked to come in for a cup of coffee, as if this was the normal thing to do. Oddly he had brought his own coffee to brew and refused to let my aunt take coffee from our pantry. He asked my aunt, "How come you speak such flawless German?"

She told him that she was originally from Germany but had come to Holland because she was Jewish and it had become increasingly difficult for Jews to live in Germany. He said that was very true, but that he had no problem with the fact that she was Jewish and we should not be afraid—the German army would not harm us. Then he turned around and asked me my age. I told him, "Eight years old." He told me that he had a son my age. After this he explained that he was part of a motorcycle unit parked across the road. He asked me to look out of the window and let him know when his unit started to move. Even though this German soldier was very polite and civilized, I was hoping that his unit would move soon because I did not like him in the house. Because of Kristallnacht, I sensed things would be bad for us Jews now that the Germans had invaded Holland. A short while later when the soldier had to leave he said goodbye and good luck.

I have often wondered at his politeness, going as far as bringing his own coffee and wishing us well. My experience with German soldiers with few exceptions would be that, at best, they did not care, but usually they would be very brutal and uncivilized. For a child, these experiences were confusing; I was never sure what to expect from my encounters with German soldiers.

Gennep was under German control almost immediately. Because Holland was supposed to be a neutral country, it had only a small army, and after five days the army surrendered. Rotterdam had been bombed, with many civilian casualties, as a warning not to resist the invaders. At the *Grebbelinie* (Grebbe Line), a defensive line to protect the major northern cities, there had been heavy casualties on both sides. The Dutch government and the Queen managed to flee to England, after the commander in chief of the Dutch army warned them that he could no longer protect them. They fled to England, leaving instructions to government employees and the civil service who remained to cooperate with the Germans in order to make life easier for the local population.

In Gennep which was close to the border with Germany, Dutch soldiers were surprised by the sudden and ferocious onslaught of the German Army. Many left their posts and, in order not to be captured and to fight again another day, took off their uniforms and put on civilian clothing borrowed from the local population. I remember seeing young men in ill-fitting street clothing standing around and staring helplessly at the German invaders. The Germans laughed at them when they saw them because they did look very strange. I often wondered when they ridiculed them whether they suspected that these young men had been Dutch soldiers.

As it turned out, the girl next door, whom I used to play with and who had tried to convert me, had an uncle, a Fifth Columnist—a covert collaborator, in fact, a German spy. Her parents had been secret members of the *Nationaal Socialistische*

Beweging (*NSB*), National Socialist Movement or Dutch Nazi party. Very early that morning some German soldiers came to pick up her uncle. Some neighbors told me that even though he was a traitor, the German soldiers despised him.

I did not know this right away, but my uncle had disappeared during the night. He went into hiding the day of the invasion because he knew that the Gestapo, the Nazi secret police, would be looking for him because he had been on their "most wanted" list before he fled Germany. Sure enough, just three days after the invasion, there was a different kind of knock on the door. It was the Gestapo looking for my uncle. They searched the house for him. When they could not find him, they took my aunt with them to question her at Gestapo headquarters.

My uncle managed to survive by always being a few steps ahead of the Gestapo and changing hiding places many times. My aunt was released by the Gestapo after they had beaten her, and once they realized that she really did not know where my uncle was.

On June 6, 1940, my grandfather, Louis Spiegel, who had been living with us, suddenly died. I remember being very upset and going to the funeral at the small Jewish cemetery. I had to say *Kaddish*, the Jewish prayer for the dead; I was the only male relative at the funeral, for Uncle Adolf had already gone into hiding to avoid capture by the Gestapo. I had difficulty saying the prayer because I was crying so much.

Then my cousin Alice, eleven years old at the time, was sick again, only this time it seemed even more serious. Alice died in July of 1940, just a few months before her twelfth birthday.

After my cousin's death, my uncle arranged for Aunt Martha and Margot to go into hiding.

CHAPTER SIX: GENNEP

The Soldiers' Song

How noble and good everyone would be if, at the end of each day,
they were to review their own behavior and weigh up the rights and
wrongs. They would automatically try to do better at the start of each
new day and, after a while, would certainly accomplish a great deal.
—*Diary of a Young Girl*, "July 15, 1944," Anne Frank

More than sixty years after the invasion of Holland, I can still hear the German soldiers sing their songs. The invasion and conquest of Holland had been easy, relatively bloodless—all over in five days. The German soldiers were happy and content, hoping and dreaming that the war would soon be over and they could go home.

Those first few weeks after the invasion, thousands of German soldiers were stationed in or near Gennep. I was eight years old and to me it seemed that the whole German army was encamped in and around Gennep. It was late spring and the days were long. We could hear them sing, especially in the evening when it was quiet. Of course they sang in German, which I understood well. Somehow I remember part of one song, because it was always sung a lot towards the end of the evening: "*Lebe wohl mein Schatz, lebe wohl, lebe wohl, denn wir fahren gegen Engeland.*" "Be well my sweetheart, be well, be well, because we will be marching against England."

This would be repeated several times with much enthusiasm. As young kids do, we would approach the nearest encampment and watch and listen to the soldiers singing. Usually one of the soldiers would get up and give each of us a piece of chocolate or a candy. Those first few weeks were like a honeymoon. The German occupiers treated the Dutch as "favorite cousins." Once England surrendered, they thought everything would be fine and soon the war would be over. Life seemed almost normal except for the German troops, and even the Jews, especially the Dutch Jews thought maybe our fears were exaggerated. I even remember one evening going with some friends to a German encampment and while one of the soldiers was giving us some candy, one of the kids pointed at me and said, "You know he's a Jew. Don't give him any candy." The German soldier answered, "Mind your own business" and gave me an extra piece of candy.

After a few weeks, most of the soldiers left, not to march against England as their favorite song went, but to march east, to prepare to attack the Soviet Union. We did not know this at the time. Other things also changed; the "honeymoon" was over very quickly, especially for us Jews. I was very unhappy about the German invasion, and despite my curiosity, I did not like seeing all those German soldiers. Yet, despite all the traumas I suffered in the years to come, I often wondered what happened to them, so happy at that time. How many, if any, survived the war? It is difficult to understand that many later took part in the atrocities committed against not only the Jews but also the general population of Europe controlled by the Germans. What would have happened if, instead of attacking the Soviet Union in 1941, they had "marched" against England and been successful?

After the German invasion in May and my grandfather's death in June and also because my Aunt Martha and cousin Margot were very busy trying to take care of Alice, my sister and I were sent to our Uncle Max and Aunt Paula in Dinxperlo in the middle of June 1940.

Uncle Max and Aunt Paula's

No it could never happen here,
Don't worry so – you'll see – it could.
                    —"Europe, Late," Dan Pagis

In June 1940, Edith and I arrived by bus in Dinxperlo, on the German border opposite the Rhine/Ruhr industrial area. My uncle and his family had been living in this village since 1935.

The first time I remember visiting my Uncle Max Spiegel and Aunt Paula was in 1938. That year my uncle and aunt had given a wedding reception for my Aunt Erna, one of my mother's sisters. Her future husband, Alwin, was already living in Palestine, but had returned to Holland in order to marry Erna. The wedding had taken place in Enschede at the Weijels', but my very generous Uncle Max had invited everybody for a reception in Dinxperlo. I remember there were a lot of people and a lot of food, and everybody was happy. I was the youngest child there and everybody spoiled me. Very soon I was tired, the trip from Dinslaken had taken a long time, and I fell asleep. Somebody carried me upstairs to the room where I was to sleep. I remember waking up several times and listening to everybody laughing and being happy.

Times were not happy by 1940. My life had changed dramatically—separation from my mother and the beginning of the war. Yet I did start school in Dinxperlo and through the efforts of my cousins, Alfred, nine years old, and Ruth, sixteen, I started to feel at home and made many new friends.

Because Dinxperlo was a small village, the German occupation of Holland did not affect our daily routine much, even though many anti-Jewish laws started to take effect and many more were to come later. By then the British air raids had begun by night, bombing the industrial cities in Germany. We could hear the air raid sirens from across the border and often the siren on top of the post office would sound, and some stray bombs would fall near our village.

Many of my friends were Jewish, such as Isaac Menist and his younger sister Jetty, Susie Gruenbaum, a next door neighbor of the Menist family, Bob Prins and his cousin Jannie Prins, who lived in Villa Pol, right across the street from us. I had also many non-Jewish friends, for example, Willy Lieber, the son of the postmaster (the post office was very close to our house), Henk Lammers, and also Harry Piepers. Henk lived three houses away. Uncle Max had rented rooms from Henk's family for three old aunts, who had arrived after *Kristallnacht* with nowhere to go. My Aunt Paula cooked their meals, and I sometimes brought these meals and stayed around to talk with Henk. Harry Piepers I remember because his brother, Richard, was goalie for the local soccer team.

There was an active branch of the NSB (Dutch Nazi Party) in Dinxperlo, trying to spread their brand of antisemitism, and their children sometimes would come to school dressed in black uniforms with big swastikas on them. However, most of the other kids tried to ignore them; they were not very popular in our school. But in general there was no discrimination yet.

Dinxperlo, on the German border, was separated from the German village of Suderwick by a huge barbed wire fence. After school we sometimes went to the street on the border to scream insults at the kids on the German side. The Dutch called the Germans "*Moffen.*" I didn't know what that meant, but I happily participated in screaming these insults at the German kids. (I later found out it meant "Jerries.") German soldiers were standing nearby at the border crossing but they ignored us.

Meanwhile the Germans continued to add new anti-Jewish laws. Everybody in the Netherlands had to have an identity card, but ours had a big "J" for *Jood*, or Jew, stamped on it. We could no longer shop in non-Jewish stores. Two houses down the road from us was the village bakery, where we had previously bought bread and rolls. Now we had to do this surreptitiously through the back door early in the morning. In addition, we were not allowed to use public transportation except by special permit, we had to surrender our bicycles, we could no longer go to the cinema, and on park benches there were signs—"Jews and dogs not allowed." Then on May 3, 1942, we had to start wearing the Jewish star, the six-pointed yellow star with the word *Jood* (Jew) written on it. If Jews were caught outside their homes without the star on their outer clothing, they were immediately sent to a concentration camp.

Already in January of that year we had been expelled from school. Jews could no longer go to the same school as non-Jews. Jewish teachers had been expelled before that because they did not want Jewish teachers to teach non-Jews. Dinxperlo had a small Jewish community with a synagogue, but it was too small to support a Jewish school. Therefore, we had to go to the nearby town Doetinchem, where a Jewish school was established for the town and the neighboring villages.

Because we were no longer going to school with all the other children, I started to lose contact with many of my former classmates. Moreover, most non-Jewish students did not make an effort to stay in touch with us or play with us. We were being separated from the rest of the population. We continued to go to school in Doetinchem all of 1942, except during summer vacations, when I went to visit my uncle and aunt, the Weijels, in Enschede.

The Family Weijel

I found neither uncle nor aunt,
I did not see my cousins either,
But I remember,
        remember
                to this day,
How their neighbors,
           looking down at the ground,
Said to me quietly: they were burnt.
        —"Burnt," Boris Slutsky

During summer vacations in 1941 and 1942, we visited Enschede to see another aunt, uncle, and cousin, as well as my maternal grandfather and grandmother. My Aunt Grete, or Margarete, my mother's youngest sister, had married Hertog Weijel, a Dutch Jew in 1935. They lived in Enschede, Holland, a prosperous textile town, close to the German border. Hertog owned a large butcher shop in Enschede together with his brothers and some other family members.

The shop prospered and Hertog and his bride had a beautiful house in Enschede. They had one child, a son Abraham Julius, born November 20, 1937. I remember the house well because I used to visit my aunt and uncle frequently and always had a good time. I remember going to visit them after their son Abraham, or Brammie as they called him, was born. By that time, a cousin of Uncle Hertog's, Mina Weijel, had moved in with them to help with the household and the baby. After

Kristallnacht, my maternal grandfather, Julius Berghausen, left his hometown, Petershagen in Germany, and came with his second wife Sophie to live in Enschede.

I remember especially the last visit in the summer of 1942. Traveling had become much more difficult; public transportation was limited because there was no gasoline. Jews had to get special permits to travel. So I was surprised one day to see Uncle Hertog in Dinxperlo, inviting Edith and me to spend the summer with them. This made me very happy and in the middle of June we arrived in Enschede to stay for about two months. By that time Brammie was four and a half years old and totally spoiled but fun to be with. Even though we stayed at my uncle and aunt's house, we also spend a lot of time with our grandparents, Julius and Sophie.

Aunt Grete and Uncle Hertog seemed to think that nothing would ever happen to them because they were Dutch. They felt it would really only affect German Jewish refugees living in Holland. By that time, my uncle, together with other Jewish men, was forced by the German authorities to guard the telephone and electric wires at night outside the town. This was in reprisal for somebody in the resistance having cut those wires. I remember him coming home in the morning, saying, "It is nothing, nobody bothered us." He seemed to be sure that this was the worst that would happen and that he and his family would not be touched.

We stayed in Enschede until the end of August, returning to Dinxperlo in time to return to school. When I said goodbye to Brammie, my uncle, aunt, and grandparents, I thought it would be a long time before I could visit them again. Little did I realize I would never see them again. Sometime at the end of September, just a month after we left, there was a *Razzia*, or roundup, at night in Enschede during which my Aunt Margarete, her son Brammie, and Mina Weijel were picked up and sent to the transit camp, Westerbork, a site where Jews were gathered for deportation to the east.

Somewhere in the dark, Uncle Hertog was out guarding the

wires, unaware of what was happening to his family. When he got home in the morning, he found his family gone and neighbors told him what had happened. He then went frantically to the local police and asked to be sent to Westerbork to be with his family. This was refused until finally in January 1943 he was sent to Westerbork.

All this I found out a few weeks later, because neighbors of my uncle came to visit family in Dinxperlo and told us everything. Of course they did not know that when my uncle arrived in Westerbork, his wife, young son, and Mina had long since been deported to Auschwitz. According to the records they were sent to Auschwitz on October 9, 1942, and killed immediately upon their arrival on October 12. My cousin Brammie was not quite five years old at the time. Uncle Hertog was sent to Auschwitz on January 28, 1943 and gassed immediately upon arrival on January 31. I am sure that upon arrival in Westerbork he volunteered to be deported east to the "resettlement or work camps," as was supposedly the destination of those trains, hoping to find his family there.

My grandfather and his wife managed to go into hiding, but unfortunately the day they went into hiding he suffered a heart attack and died. Julius is buried in the Jewish cemetery in Enschede. My step-grandmother Sophie survived in hiding. I was able to visit her several times after the war. She told me what had happened, how she and my grandfather tried to persuade Hertog and Grete to go into hiding, at least for their child's sake. However, my aunt and uncle believed that it was much too dangerous to go into hiding and that their Dutch nationality would protect them. All of my Uncle Hertog's immediate family, including his brothers, was murdered in Auschwitz.

CHAPTER NINE: DINXPERLO

Letters from My Mother

Escaped from Germany—
Cared for by English friends, with whom
Kindness counted still—

Rumors reached her—

Photographs made by the Gestapo—

Jews, her people—
        —"History and Reality," Stephen Spender

The following are some letters Edith and I received in Dinxperlo from and to my mother in England. She was only allowed to write a few words and we were only allowed to respond briefly. A maximum of twenty-five words was permitted and we could only write about family and personal matters. The British Red Cross saw to it that we received these letters and that she received ours.

It usually took three to four months before these letters reached their destination.

Leeds, June 19, 1941
Dear All,
Hope you are all well and happy. I am fine. I have a very good job.
Regards and kisses, Elise.

Dinxperlo, October 29, 1941
Dear Elise:
Dinxperlo, Gennep, all well. Children on vacation in
Enschede. Edith can swim, bicycle. Both excellent school
reports. All the best for the New Year, Paula, Max.

The reply to my mother's first letter by my Uncle Max is very interesting because in twenty-five words he managed to cover everything.

The above letter and reply, translated from the original German, was the first of a series of International Red Cross letters my sister and I were to receive until the final letter we wrote in December 1942. At that time I was ten years old, and my sister, fourteen.

I found these letters, after my mother passed away, among other documents she had saved all those years. These letters brought back many memories of a different time and a different world many years ago.

After the invasion of Holland, she had no way to get in touch with us. At the urging of some friends, this first letter was sent as an inquiry through the war organization of the British Red Cross and Order of St. John, Prisoner of War, Wounded and Missing Department. There had apparently been no precedent until then for getting in touch with somebody. I would guess that the millions of Jews stranded on the continent of Europe did not warrant any special department. This inquiry was forwarded to the International Red Cross in Geneva, from there to the German Red Cross, and finally to the Dutch Red Cross. When we replied, this procedure was reversed. This way, contact was established and my mother received a number of letters from us and other family members starting in the latter part of 1941 until the end of 1942. Only the letters we sent in reply to her letters, and letters sent to her by other family members, survived.

The following few letters stand out and I would like to share them with you.

Dinxperlo, February 24, 1942
Dear Mother,
Received letter. Fritz and I and everybody are fine. We are
remaining here. Please write a lot. We have grown tall and
strong.
Thousand kisses, Edith.

Leeds, March 3, 1942
Dear Children,
Best wishes for your birthdays, dear children. Hope that you
and Aunt Paula and family well. Why no news from
Gennep?
Regards and kisses, Mother.

Leeds, April 27, 1942
Dear Children,
Letter received, why not there? I am happy everybody is
well. I am fine. Reply soon.
Regards and kisses, Mother.

Leeds, September 8, 1942
Dear Children,
Happy received your letter. Glad everybody is well. Please
let children write themselves. Write often. I am fine. Regards
to everybody.
Kisses, Mother.

Dinxperlo, October 28, 1942
Dear Mother,
Very happy to receive your letter. Fritz, myself, everybody
fine. You also should write a lot. We are going to school.
Kisses, Edith and Fritz.

Leeds, October 13, 1942
Dear Children.
Hope you and everybody well. Please, children, write often.
Received letter from Aunt Grete and Grandma.
Regards and kisses, Mother.

Our final reply:

Dinxperlo December 30, 1942
Dear Mother,
Happy to receive your letter. We and all relatives in Holland
fine. We are on vacation. We grew a lot. I am tall as Aunt
Paula.
A thousand kisses, Edith, Fritz

These letters often crossed as it took three to four months to receive them. What agony my mother must have suffered those many years ago because after this final letter, there was nothing. She tried to send many more letters, but there was nobody to receive them. There were only rumors about what was happening and these rumors were not comforting.

Meanwhile, Edith and I continued living with Uncle Max and Aunt Paula in Dinxperlo and going to the Jewish school in Doetinchem.

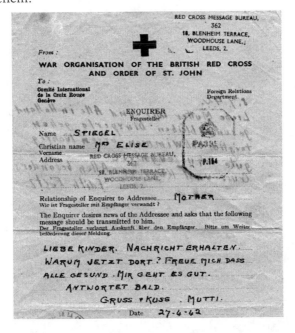

The Jewish School

A nothing
we were, are, shall
remain, flowering;
the nothing-, the
no one's rose.
    —"Psalm," Paul Celan

I n 1942, a new law expelled all Jewish children from public schools in Holland. This included Dinxperlo. I had been going to the local school with my cousin Alfred, and I had made a lot of friends. So it was rather difficult suddenly to leave everything I had been used to. Many of the students and teachers were also unhappy that the Jewish children had to leave or rather be expelled.

We had to wear the yellow six-pointed star with the word *Jood* on our clothes. But aside from that we were pretty much left alone. This was not the case in the larger cities, such as Amsterdam, Rotterdam, and The Hague, where there were curfews, where Jews were not allowed on public transportation and where park benches had signs reading, "Jews and dogs not allowed." During the *Razzia*, the local police would round up Jews and send them to the transit camp, Westerbork, and from there to "work or resettlement camps" in the East. But this was not yet a part of life here.

We did have to go to a separate school, however. Unhappily, the small number of children involved did not warrant the establishment of a Jewish school in Dinxperlo. Doetinchem, about twenty-five kilometers from Dinxperlo, was a small city, centrally located, and a Jewish school was established there to serve the city and all the surrounding villages. The big question was: How would we travel there? Jews were no longer allowed on public transportation, except by special permit. Also there were hardly any buses out of Dinxperlo to anywhere. The problem was solved in a unique way. Some days we went by bus, but most of the time we went together by horse and cart to a small place called Bonte Brug, on the main road, where buses stopped regularly on the way to Doetinchem. By that time in 1942 no gasoline was available; the German army had taken all. Each bus had a huge stove at the back, which burned wood, and the fumes made the bus go. This did not function well, and we broke down often, but somehow we made it almost every day.

At the beginning about a hundred children attended the school at Doetinchem. We had very good teachers because Jewish teachers had not been permitted to work and teach in the regular schools for quite some time. For a while it was fun traveling to Doetinchem. However, we were away from home usually about ten hours—a long day. But I made a lot of new friends, and local Jewish families invited us for lunch. The family I went to had an older daughter, Sonja (not her real name; I cannot remember hers or her family's name), a gifted student, who played the piano very well, which fascinated me. So she tried to teach me to play the piano every afternoon.

A few weeks after we started to travel to Doetinchem, the Nazis began *Razzias*, rounding up Jews from the cities and sending them to the transit camp, Westerbork, a site where Jews were gathered for transit to the east. During these roundups, they would cordon off an area of the city at night and then go from apartment to apartment and house to house. If there were Jews living there, they had twenty minutes to pack a few belongings and go to a waiting truck, which would then take them to a central location and from there by train to Westerbork. Every week there were fewer children in the school. Some went into hiding with their parents, though we did not know about this because knowing this was very dangerous. Nobody really knew if and when anybody went into hiding. Unfortunately, very few did.

One morning in November 1942, Sonja did not come to school. Nobody seemed to know what had happened to her. I was very upset because I had become very attached to her; she was like an older sister to me. I went to her house at lunchtime, but the door was locked and nobody was there. The house was empty. I looked through the windows. Even the furniture was gone, including the piano. In the afternoon I was told by one of the teachers that there had been a *Razzia* the previous night. What was worse, Sonja had been picked up from the street by the Nazis in late afternoon, while she was walking home. That same evening Sonja was sent alone to Westerbork. Her parents, who went to look for her that night, were also arrested and sent to Westerbork the next day. But Sonja never saw her parents again. She was transported on to Auschwitz the morning after her arrival. She was fifteen years old at the time, and apparently upon her arrival in Auschwitz she was selected to work.

According to what I was told, she died in Auschwitz in the beginning of 1944—not yet seventeen years old. Her parents were transported to Auschwitz a week after arriving in Westerbork. Upon their arrival in Auschwitz, they were killed in the gas chambers.

The school was closed at the end of 1942. By that time there were hardly any children left.

CHAPTER ELEVEN: DINXPERLO

The Prins Family

> *Terrible nursemaids*
> *Have usurped the place of mothers.*
> —"O the Night of the Weeping Children!" Nelly Sachs

When I was still traveling by bus to Doetinchem to the Jewish school, I had a strange and terrible experience on one of those trips, in the early fall of 1942. I have never forgotten this bus ride.

On this particular morning I arrived at the bus station and got on the bus. There sitting in the back of the bus was Maurits Prins, his wife, Bertha, and their three children, Philip, Carolina, and Jannie, each one sitting next to a policeman. Apparently at dawn the Gestapo and the local police had raided Villa Pol, where the Prins family lived. They had to leave their home immediately; they were not allowed to take anything with them or even to wash and dress properly. The police then decided to take them by local bus to Doetinchem. The ride was at least an hour because there were many stops and the bus went very slowly. I managed to sit in the seat just in front of Jannie. I knew the Prins family well because Villa Pol was opposite my uncle's house. I was friendly with Jannie, a few years older than I. I remember talking to her all the way to Doetinchem and she kept reassuring me that all this was just a big mistake and that she and her family would be back soon once everything was straightened out. The policeman sitting next to her never said a word, but Jannie complained that she had not even been able to wash her face and put some makeup on. Upon arrival in Doetinchem they got off the bus after us, and I watched them slowly walk away towards the police station. I did say goodbye to Jannie and that I hoped to see her that evening or the next day back in Dinxperlo. But I never saw them again. A few days later some of their workers came to the Villa Pol to pack some clothes for the family, who by then were in Westerbork.

In contrast, on this same day, the family of Leopold Prins, a cousin of Maurits, who also lived in Dinxperlo, was picked up and put in a truck. Then they were taken across the border into Germany to be interrogated before being sent to Westerbork and then later to Auschwitz.

Both the Prins families were very prominent and well known in Dinxperlo and the surrounding area. Both families, who were wealthy and lived on beautiful, large estates, were involved in many communal activities. The Villa Pol had a very large yard, where nearly every day the bigger boys of the village played a very tough game of soccer with Maurits Prins, a good player himself. Apparently they had been planning to go into hiding but somebody in the village whom they trusted had betrayed them.

The events of that day will always remain with me, especially the memory of sitting on the seat in front of Jannie, while she was trying to reassure me and probably herself that everything would be fine and that I could come and see her at home that evening or the next day.

For over fifty years I have wondered whether my memory of this event was correct, whether this incident really happened this way. Usually the police would come to Jewish houses or apartments and take them by trucks to an assembly point and when they had a big enough transport would send them by train—usually to Westerbork.

So it is still a mystery to me what happened that day, why the family Prins had to endure this special kind of torture, to travel on a regularly scheduled bus full of regular passengers to their doom.

Jannie, her sister, Caroline, and their mother, Bertha, were killed in Auschwitz on October 26, 1942. Maurits died in Neukirch on June 30, 1943. His son Philip died in Ludwigsdorf on January 1, 1944.

CHAPTER TWELVE: DINXPERLO

Allied Air Raids

Above—in a death swordplay, metal pirates
Spit whistling arrows into the heart of the moon.
    —"Faces in Swamps IV," Abraham Sutzkever

J ust across the border from Dinxperlo was the Rhine/Ruhr industrial area with its many cities like Emmerich and Bocholt and a little further away Cologne. Because of its heavy industry, this area became a prime target for Allied bombers, starting with the British at night and months later the American bombers during the day.

We had many heavy nightly raids by British bombers, aiming for the industrial area. Sometimes bombs that missed their target hit our village, or debris from aircraft shot down landed on us. If it had not been so dangerous and deadly, it would have made a great "sound and light show," with tracer bullets, searchlights, and fiery airplanes lighting the night sky for miles around.

Our house was not far away from the post office on whose roof was the siren that gave the alarm when bombers came near.

Dinxperlo was not a target, but neighboring Germany was, and as soon as the sirens in the German towns started to wail, the siren on our post office joined in and woke everybody up. The first few months I used to turn around to go back to sleep, but my sister would try to convince me to sit downstairs with my uncle, aunt, and cousins Ruth and Alfred, until the raid was over. Sometimes the bombing got quite heavy and came very close. Everything used to shake and in my sleep I could actually hear the heavy bombs scream and whistle. Nobody in the village had a shelter, so we could do very little about it anyway.

As the months went by, the raids became heavier. Hundreds of heavy bombers used to cross our village. The Germans had placed searchlights and anti-aircraft guns in the area and started to shoot down some of the airplanes. At the same time, German fighter planes came from the opposite direction and the sky above our village at night became a battlefield. Bombers that had been hit attempted to remain airborne by releasing their heavy load of bombs. It became almost impossible to sleep and very dangerous as fiery airplanes were crashing from the skies and bombs were falling on the village.

We had been lucky; very few houses had been hit. Most bombs fell in open fields, leaving huge craters. Bits and pieces of airplanes scattered everywhere. Sometimes some of the crew managed to bail out, but usually, the Germans immediately took them prisoners. A few landed with local farmers who at great risk managed to hide them. More often the crews, especially the pilots, were killed. The next day the German army would give them military funerals, which I never quite understood, because to the Germans they were the enemy.

By the spring of 1942, the only time it was quiet and peaceful was when the weather was too bad for flying. The Americans had started daylight raids, and it seemed to me that everybody who wanted to bomb Germany had to cross the skies above our village. Sometimes when the night raid was over, the day raid started. Yet Dinxperlo had very few casualties.

Despite the continuing and random bombardments, Dinxperlo managed to escape heavy damage and casualties until March 1945. According to Willy Lieber's book, *Oorlog in de Achtertuin* (*War in the Backyard*), and A. J. Lammers' book, *Dinxperlo in Oorlogstijd* (*Dinxperlo in War Time*), the British army, approaching from across the German border, was met by heavy resistance from German troops stationed in Dinxperlo and the vicinity. The village had been shelled several times from the middle of March on. The last five days of March are remembered as Dinxperlo's darkest days with constant heavy shelling. By Good Friday, March 30, the German army retreated. The village and the surrounding area were badly damaged with many civilian deaths. Most of the villagers had lived in shelters to protect themselves. On March 31, 1945, the 51st Highland Division of the British army finally liberated Dinxperlo.

Yom Kippur Eve, 1942

Vainly would you look for lighted candles in windows,
And listen for chanting from a wooden synagogue.
                    —"Elegy," Antoni Slonimski

O n *Yom Kippur* (Day of Atonement) Eve 1942, the Jewish year of 5703, the village's and my sense of security changed dramatically. I went to the synagogue that evening, together with my cousin Alfred, for *Yom Kippur* Eve Services, called *Kol Nidrei,* when prayers are said and songs are sung at sunset. Uncle Max did not feel well, so he did not come with us. We arrived at the synagogue, crowded with men wearing the traditional white robes for *Yom Kippur.* As was the custom, the women were sitting upstairs.

Suddenly, just as the cantor started chanting the *Kol Nidrei,* a young man came running into the synagogue shouting, "The Gestapo is coming to arrest all the Jewish men. They're sending them to a concentration camp called Mauthausen." The cantor stopped his prayers and there was a deadly silence in the congregation. No one panicked, but slowly, as if by previous arrangement or as in a bad dream, the men started to take off their white robes. While the cantor was praying, they left one by one. Once outside nobody ran, but I could see them through the open door walking fast and furtively towards their homes, taking detours and disappearing into the twilight. The cantor continued to pray, but soon there was nobody left except my cousin, a few other young boys, and me. I don't remember seeing any women upstairs either, so they must have left to be with their husbands and fathers. The cantor then turned to us: "Would you please go home, I must leave now." With that he left the synagogue, together with us, and we could just see the last of the men disappearing into the autumn dusk.

This was the last time that there was a service in the synagogue of Dinxperlo.

I never saw any members of that congregation again.

A memorial to the vanished congregation with the names of all the members who were killed was put up a few years ago in the place where the synagogue once stood. Unfortunately nearly all the names of my childhood friends of those years in Dinxperlo are on this memorial. For over fifty years I have not gone to synagogue for Kol Nidrei services on Yom Kippur Eve.

A few months after this "incident," in April 1943, a new law went into effect that the provinces of Holland had to be *Judenrein* (cleansed of Jews). Except for those few who managed to go into hiding, most of the Jewish population of Dinxperlo was sent to the slave labor/concentration camp Vught in the south of Holland. From Vught nearly everybody was sent to Westerbork and then on to the various concentration and death camps.

Of those only four survived. The Dinxperlo synagogue was destroyed during a bombardment, and no Jews live there today. A congregation of fifty to sixty members disappeared.

On April 10, 1943, Edith and I were forced to leave Dinxperlo. Together with my Uncle Max's family we were sent to Vught. We were picked up early in the morning and taken by truck to the railroad station in Nijmegen. From there we went the rest of the way to Vught by train.

When we left Dinxperlo for Vught, most of the rest of the population of the village stood there and watched. Many of them were "bystanders." Although a few by then were active in the resistance, they could have done very little to help us, except to hide us, which would have been too dangerous.

My sister was almost happy to leave the constant bombardments. She had no idea what lay ahead.

PART III

The Camps, 1943-45

And praised. Auschwitz. Be. Majdanek. The Lord. Treblinka. And
praised. Buchenwald. Be. Mauthausen. The Lord. Belzec. And
praised. Sobibor. Be. Chelmno. The Lord. Ponary. And praised.
Theresienstadt. Be. Warsaw. The Lord. Vilna. And praised.
Skarzysko. Be. Bergen-Belsen. The Lord. Janow. And praised. Dora.
Be. Neuengamme. The Lord. Pustkow. And praised ....
　　　　　　　—"The Last of the Just," Andre Schwarz-Bart

CHAPTER FOURTEEN: VUGHT, NETHERLANDS

A Day in a Camp

Where is the child
To fill those shoes
Why has the bride
Gone barefoot?
  —"A Cartload of Shoes," Abraham Sutzkever

Our train arrived in Vught at the beginning of April 1943. Vught was near a branch of the Philips Electronic factories, which the Germans considered vital to the war effort. I was almost eleven years old at the time and was together with my sister Edith, my Uncle Max, Aunt Paula, and my cousins, Alfred and Ruth.

Upon our arrival in Vught, we very soon learned what a concentration camp was. We were put in the Jewish segment of the camp, called *Judendurchgangslager Vught,* or *Jewish Transit Camp Vught,* even though it was a work or slave labor camp. Children were torn away from their parents and relatives. I could not see my uncle and aunt because we were not allowed to go to their barracks. Along with Alfred, I was in a barracks for boys only. Edith was in a different barracks with other girls.

What were young children doing in a slave labor camp? There is no answer to that. I was eleven years old; many of the children were a lot younger. Some of the adults in the camp attempted to organize a school of sorts. However, because they had to go to work, this was not successful. We were left to languish, at the mercy of the guards who sometimes beat us or otherwise abused us. Although most children were in the camp with their parents who tried very hard to protect them, this was difficult because children were in separate barracks. Once in a while, some of the parents and relatives were allowed to see their children. Yet to see their children suffer under these very harsh conditions was painful and frustrating for them. Also the barracks leaders, themselves prisoners, did their utmost to protect the children, but they could not protect them from hunger and disease.

Aside from the Jews, others were imprisoned in Vught, mostly men. Some wore red triangles on their clothing, meaning that they had been active in the resistance; the Germans considered anybody active in the resistance a Communist, hence, the red triangle. Some prisoners wore black triangles because they had been caught dealing in the "black market." Some wore pink triangles for homosexuals, called "asocials." We Jews wore our Jewish star.

During the month of April 1943 when I arrived with many other children, more people were coming in every day than were leaving, thus the camp was over crowded. By the beginning of May 1943 about 1800 Jewish children were in Vught. Every morning there was roll call. Children too had to go to these roll calls. Only those children who were very sick were excused. After a lot of screaming and yelling, the adults were marched off to work. Then the children were dismissed, and we ran to our barracks, with some of the guards chasing us. Nobody seemed to know why we were there or what to do with us.

Some prisoners, mostly members of the resistance, tried to escape. If they were caught, they were severely beaten, sent to isolation cells, or sometimes shot. This was our introduction to a concentration camp. It was frightening, especially for children.

We received very little food and some of it was rotten. However, Aunt Paula had prepared our luggage months in advance in case we would be taken to a camp and she made sure we had some food with us, mainly dried fruits, some canned food and some cookies and crackers. Upon our arrival we were allowed to keep this food, which helped to supplement our diet for a few weeks. Some families with children had arrived several weeks before us, mostly from the larger cities; they had been picked up at night during the *Razzias*. They brought very little with them and they were completely dependent upon the camp rations. Many of those children, especially the younger ones, became very sick and some died mainly of malnutrition.

I remember being afraid most of the time and so were the other children. Things became worse by the day and many more children became sick—some because of the lice. Lice carried diseases, so we were periodically deloused. This was a terrifying experience. The guards showed then how cruel they could be.

One morning, about three weeks after our arrival, was more terror filled than usual. At roll call, we were told that we were going to be deloused and our clothing disinfected because, according to the Germans, we were all filthy and covered in lice. We had to bring all our clothing to one barrack that was sealed and there our clothing would be disinfected. Next we had to undress, and this clothing also was put in another barrack. We then had to run naked to the shower, quite a distance away, and it was cold outside. After the shower we had to walk back to a different barrack, even further away, where we were told our clothing had been moved for some unknown reason.

I had not been aware that the girls, separate from us in the girls' barracks, had also been forced to undress under the watchful eyes of the camp guards. Suddenly while we were walking towards the barrack to get our clothing, we saw a group of naked girls running towards us, screaming, with guards running after them. They started to pass us and were embarrassed when they saw us and tried to look away. I noticed that most of them were crying and many of the girls seemed to have marks all over their bodies. Then suddenly one of the girls stopped and screamed my name. She was crying. She was Jetty Menist, who, together with her older brother Isaac, was a close friend of mine from Dinxperlo. She threw her hands into the air and said, "Look at me, just look at me. See what they did to me." I saw that her body was covered with wounds. All this happened in a few seconds, but to me it seemed like an eternity.

Apparently the camp guards had attacked and abused many of these girls, who were between the ages of six and fourteen. I saw Jetty again that same evening, from a distance, because we were not allowed to come near the girls' barracks. She was sitting down with the other girls, eating what little food we had received. She was dressed and seemed to have calmed down. She did not see me. I never saw her again after that. Because we had been very close friends that incident and the terror in her face always remained with me. I always wondered, "Why did she call my name and not her brother Isaac's?"

For me, there was never really "closure" on this incident. I did not quite understand at the time what Jetty was trying to tell me. Only years later did I begin to realize what had happened to her and many of the other young girls that day in Vught.

In May, more families were called and put on transports to Westerbork. On May 23, 1943, after spending about six weeks from April 10 to May 23 in Vught, my name was called, together with my sister's, and my uncle's family, except for my cousin Ruth, who was older and working as a slave laborer in the nearby Philips Electronics factory. I was very happy to leave Vught. The last few weeks at Vught had been brutal. The SS guards and the camp police had constantly harassed us. There was very little food and tremendous overcrowding. Our destination was transit camp Westerbork where I hoped life would be less cruel. I was wishing for better things ahead.

On June 6 and 7, 1943, the 1269 children remaining in Vught together with their families were transported to Westerbork. The next day, June 8, all of them were put on a train eastbound for the death camp of Sobibor, Poland. Jetty was on that transport with her family. They were all gassed immediately upon arrival on June 11. She was only nine and a half years old at the time.

Transit Camp

> They are sorted and marked—the method is up to you.
> The books must be balanced, the disposition stated.
> Take care that all accounts are neat and true.
>
> Make sure that they are thoroughly cremated.
>   —"Shipment to Maidanek," Ephraim Fogel

We were assembled early on the morning of May 23, 1943, and put on a train—destination Transit Camp Westerbork. I had just turned eleven. I was with my sister Edith, fifteen years old, Uncle Max, Aunt Paula, and cousin Alfred, twelve years old.

Westerbork had been established in 1939 by the Dutch, as a camp for German Jewish refugees who had crossed the border illegally after *Kristallnacht* and had nowhere to go. It was taken over by the Germans in 1942; they considered it a perfect place for a transit camp because of its location in northeastern Holland in the middle of nowhere, near the German border, and with good railroad connections east. It had previously been well organized by the Jews themselves when the camp was under Dutch control. The Germans took over on July 1, 1942.

Westerbork was very crowded because nearly everybody had

a deferment, or exemption from being transported east to the so-called resettlement or work camps. These deferments were given for various reasons: for "essential" workers at the camp and for foreign or enemy nationals. Sometimes, with enough money, deferments could be bought. Because of this, it became difficult to fill the trains heading east every Tuesday. However, it was a transit camp, not a concentration camp, and very much better than Vught.

The problem was the weekly transports east to the "resettlement or work camps." We had noticed a very long train, consisting of cattle wagons standing on a siding. Inmates of Westerbork told us newcomers, "This is the train that takes Jews east to resettlement and work camps—every Tuesday."

The lists of those to be deported were prepared by the Jewish Council within the camp and submitted by the head of the council, Kurt Schlesinger, to the German commander, Albert Konrad Gemmeker. In order to make things easier for themselves, the *Judenraat,* or Jewish Council (Jewish leaders selected by the Nazis) often put all the people arriving the previous few days on the lists before they knew them and often before the new arrivals had the opportunity to obtain an exemption or deferment.

Soon after my arrival in Westerbork, I narrowly escaped being deported on one of these transports.

The Missed Transport

Go back into your mist.
It's not my fault if I live and breathe.
—"The Survivor," Primo Levi

We had arrived in Westerbork late Monday afternoon after about a six hour train ride, and we were immediately separated, my cousin and I in one huge barrack, my sister elsewhere, and my uncle and aunt also in different barracks. Most people in our barrack had arrived together with us. Yet our first night in Westerbork was uncomfortable. Nobody was able to sleep much that night. The barracks were huge, noisy, and very crowded; each barrack held about 500 to 1000 people. Bunks were stacked three high.

Very early in the morning, the barrack leader started to read out the names of the people to be put on the train that day. As my name and my cousin Alfred's name was called, we walked towards the train, carrying the few belongings we were allowed to take with us. It was dawn and the walk to the train was very scary. Nearly everybody was crying, especially the little children. The people not going on that train were under total curfew and could neither leave their barracks nor look out of the few windows. The only people we saw were the German SS guards with their dogs, Dutch policemen, and the Jewish camp police, or *Ordnungsdienst* (OD). I saw nobody I knew, nor anyone from my family, except Alfred.

When the OD started to push us on the train, I panicked. Everything was so crowded. Some people cried, but most went quietly onto the train. I screamed loudly, " I don't want to go onto this train." When Alfred heard me screaming, he also started to scream. This caught the attention of an SS guard who asked a Dutch policeman what the screaming was all about. He apparently answered, "I think the children are afraid and do not want to go on the train." The SS guard then immediately gave the order to take my cousin and me off that train. The same OD, who had been pushing us on, took us off, and we were put in a small room isolated from everybody else until after the train departed—without us. I did not realize at the time that I had narrowly escaped death.

As I found out years later, this was very unusual. There was always commotion when these trains left because nobody wanted to be crammed on the trains going to an unknown destination eastwards. However, it was indeed a rare occasion when a German guard ordered a Jew to be taken off a train destined for the gas chambers. The Germans preferred that the Jews went quietly and orderly. Apparently my screaming did not fit in with their plans.

Years later, I also found out that nearly everybody who had arrived from Vught the day before was on this train and sent to the death camp Sobibor in Poland. There were no survivors. Between March and August 1943, about 35,000 Jews were transported from Westerbork to Sobibor. Only nineteen people are known to have survived.

Uncle Max and Aunt Paula had not been aware that we were almost deported. Immediately upon arrival in Westerbork,

Uncle Max had applied for an exemption, not to be sent on one of those trains east. He had been a soldier in the German army in World War I and for this, for the time being, he had received an exemption. He thought this would keep all of us safe from being deported.

However, he soon realized, especially after what nearly happened to us, that his deferment would not apply to my sister and me because we were not his children. He felt it was his responsibility to try and save us. My uncle consulted with Kurt Schlesinger, the head of the Jewish council. Schlesinger suggested that my uncle put us on the so-called Weinreb deferment list. For a large amount of money paid to Weinreb, a German Jew living in Holland, people were put on a special list of people who would not be put on those transports east. My uncle was ready to do this, even though it meant that it would cost him almost all the money he still had hidden with non-Jewish friends.

Weinreb had been highly recommended because he was able to pay off the Nazis to save himself, his family, and other people who were willing to pay. My uncle decided to go ahead, but somehow at the last moment changed his mind. He then decided to go and see the German SS Camp *Kommandant*, Albert Gemmeker, even though everybody, including Kurt Schlesinger, strongly advised him against it, as this was considered very dangerous and might cost him his life. But he saw Gemmeker and tried to convince him that my sister and I were British citizens and as proof he brought with him the Red Cross letters we had received from my mother who was living in England at that time. We were foreign nationals. We had those Red Cross letters to prove it (see Chapter Nine). I was never quite sure what transpired, whether we now had deferments as British citizens or if we were still on the Weinreb list.

About six weeks after this incident, my Uncle Max's exemption expired, as all exemptions and deferments eventually did in Westerbork. My uncle, aunt, and Alfred's names were on the list to be sent east to one of those "work or resettlement" camps. I spoke to my cousin before he left and I said to him, "I will see you soon." I believed that my sister and I would probably follow them, being sent on a later transport. Alfred seemed to have a premonition that this would not happen. He was crying and said, "I don't think so." Unfortunately he was right; as I found out after the war, they were deported to Sobibor and killed in the gas chambers on July 2, 1943.

Even though he would never know, my uncle's maneuvering had succeeded in keeping us off those trains to Sobibor and Auschwitz and allowed us to stay in Westerbork.

We could remain in Westerbork for the time being as we apparently were considered "Foreign Nationals" because our mother was living in Leeds, England, as an *au pair*, a foreign maid. We would now live in the orphanage of Transit Camp Westerbork, which was still under the jurisdiction of *Kommandant* Gemmeker.

Kommandant Gemmeker

It's difficult in times like these:
ideals, dreams, cherished hopes rise within us,
only to be crushed by grim reality.
      —*Diary of a Young Girl*, "July 15, 1944, Anne Frank

Albert Konrad Gemmeker was the commander of the *Polizeiliches Judendurchgangslager* Westerbork, the Jewish transit camp Westerbork—from October 12, 1942 until April 11, 1945, the day the camp was liberated by Canadian troops. The camp was organized very similarly to a ghetto. A Jewish camp commander with a committee and Jewish camp orderlies ran the camp.

Gemmeker was a master of deception. It was essential that the camp inmates believe that when they were deported to the east that they were being relocated to a special area in the east set aside for the Jews of Europe. This new "home" would be a place where Jews could resettle, starting life anew.

In order to deceive the Jews in Westerbork, Gemmeker pretended to be a good man, a man concerned for the well-being of all the people in the camp. One example of his deception involved the theatre. Many prominent artists, actors and musicians came to Westerbork, and with the encouragement of Gemmeker they organized vibrant cultural activities. The highlight was The Cabaret, which produced many shows, the most spectacular being "Humor and Melody" in September 1943. The *Kommandant* and his aides attended these shows, and many people participating thought that maybe Gemmeker and the Nazis were humane after all. How mistaken everybody was.

Another example of Gemmeker's cruelty is recounted in a book, published in Dutch about Westerbork, by Willy Lindwer, *Kamp van Hoop en Wanhoop (Camp of Hope and Desperation)*. This book relates a story about Gemmeker, as told by Mrs. Trudel van Reemst-De Vries:

I was a nurse at the hospital in Westerbork. One day while working there I was asked by one of the nurses to come with her. And there in a small room was a little baby wrapped in rags and blankets, a real small blond baby boy. The baby had been born in the concentration camp Vught. The mother who with other women worked at the Phillips factories had been standing for an idiotic long time, twelve hours or more at roll call. She was six months pregnant at the time and gave birth during this roll call. Afterwards the women were all sent on cattle wagons to Westerbork. During the trip the women took all their clothing and wrapped it around the baby to keep it warm. Now the baby was with us in the children's section. So was the mother for a short while. Kommandant Gemmeker who was supposed to be very concerned about children ordered an incubator to be brought from Groningen, the nearest place where one was available. Not only that, he consulted with Professor Van Crefeld, a well-known pediatrician from Amsterdam, about what should be done to keep the child alive. Professor Van Crefeld came the same day, when the child was already in the incubator, to see him. The child's name was Michieltje and I will always remember this until the end of my life. The child had to be fed in a special way, as he was too weak to breastfeed or suck from a bottle.

Because he was so weak, he was fed every hour and after each feeding he was supposed to get a drop of cognac. It is unbelievable, but Gemmeker send a bottle of Hennessey cognac in order to give to the child. I became one of the two nurses responsible for the baby and naturally we did everything in our power to help the baby. The mother had in the meanwhile been sent on a transport east because she could not breastfeed the baby. Normally mothers who were breastfeeding had an exemption, for the time being, from being put on those transports.

Gemmeker came regularly to see how the baby was doing. I did not understand his interest, but it meant to us that the baby would survive. And this was with the help of Gemmeker who was our enemy. We held on to this hope and that little baby. And he became stronger and soon was able to drink out of a bottle. Later when he weighed five and a half pounds, he came out of the incubator into a crib. And Gemmeker came to have a look. We thought: we have succeeded; this is proof that there is some good in the person, that there is hope, that there is a future.

However, when Michieltje weighed six pounds, he was put on a transport east to the "work camps."

This story is symbolic of what Westerbork was like—a place of lies.

The cabaret and stage of the Westerbork Theater were also a manifestation of the absurd. The cream of Jewish talent performed for auditoriums filled with Jewish prisoners while Gemmeker and his aides sat in the front row. I never went to any of these performances because I felt uncomfortable in the presence of the Germans. Yet every Tuesday trains were bound eastwards for the journey of no return. In the end, all this talent—actors, musicians, and artists—was sent east and most of them did not return. Gemmeker was fully aware that those performances created the illusion of "normal life" within the confines of barbed wire. In the fall of 1944, all performances were stopped by order of Gemmeker and the remaining artists were sent to their death. In 1947, Gemmeker was sentenced to ten years in prison, minus the years he had already served.[7]

The Orphanage

Suddenly the Old Doctor saw
the children had grown
as old as he was
older and older
that was how fast they had to go grey as ash.
    —"5.8.1942 In Memory of Janusz Korczak," Jerzy Ficowski

The orphanage in Westerbork was established in 1939, by Mr. Jehoshua (Otto) Birnbaum, an educator from Berlin with six children of his own.[6] By the time my sister and I came to the orphanage it was crowded with orphans. Sometimes the *Gruene Polizei*, police in green uniform, in the bigger cities, especially in Amsterdam, would pick up Jewish children, without their parents, on their way to or from schools. Also many times children in hiding with non-Jewish families were betrayed and these too would arrive in Westerbork without parents.

Mr. Birnbaum was allowed to take children up to the age of fifteen. At age fifteen they would be considered adults. A lot of very young children lived in the orphanage. Mr. Birnbaum had access to the lists being prepared every week for deportation east because the Jewish Camp Council prepared these lists. If he found the name of any of "his" children on the lists, he would run to the German *Kommandant* Gemmeker and plead with him not to deport the children.

Birnbaum would tell Gemmeker that the children were much too young to go to a work or resettlement camp in the east and that he would take care of them. So for a while the *Kommandant* relented and took the children off the lists. The Jewish Camp Council created special exemption lists for the children; they were put on the so-called Palestine lists, Jews selected for possible exchange with the British for German Nationals. If chosen, these Jews would later immigrate to Palestine.

This was the situation in the orphanage and it continued for several months. It was a safe haven for us; I got used to the life there. We received a little more food than the rest of the camp, and we were allowed to receive parcels from the outside. We received non-perishable food parcels from Dinxperlo, from Mimi Otten, who was working for the resistance. My uncle had given her money before we were deported to send the food to us. We shared our parcels with the other children.

Also many prominent professors, teachers, and musicians came to help in the orphanage, before they were themselves deported. The one I remember best was Mrs. Clara Asscher Pinkhof, a well-known Jewish Dutch author of children's books. She was the widow of the rabbi of Groningen and became an author after his death. I remember her especially well because she was a good storyteller.

Then came November 16, 1943. The camp was very crowded, with about 25,000 people. It was Monday evening and the train stood ready to go east the next morning. About 2500 Jews were supposed to be deported that day. However, nearly everybody in the camp had some sort of exemption. So this time there were not enough people to fill the train. The head of the Jewish council, Kurt Schlesinger, went to Gemmeker and told him, "There are not enough people without exemptions." Then the Kommandant canceled all exemptions, including most Palestine lists. This meant that nearly all the children of the orphanage were put on the deportation lists, despite Mr. Birnbaum's efforts.

Most of the children in the orphanage, many of whom were very young, went on this train to Auschwitz and to the gas chambers. But my sister and I were saved, I assume, because my uncle, at the last moment, had changed his mind, as noted earlier, and had decided not to put us on that Weinreb list, but instead to stress the fact that our mother was in England. This all happened because Uncle Max somehow did not believe that paying money would keep us from being sent on one of those trains east. For him it was very important to save our lives because he felt that he was obliged to protect us so that we could be reunited with our mother after the war.

Many people working in the orphanage, including Mr. Birnbaum, volunteered to go with the children, even though they were not on the deportation list. They wanted to take care of the children once they had arrived at these resettlement or work camps. The *Kommandant* would not allow Mr. Birnbaum to accompany the children. So he stayed behind, as did Edith and I, among the few other children who were left.

This was a terrible night for all of us. Many of the children were very young and all of us were unhappy. We did not know what their fate would be. In the morning the train left with most of the children packed into cattle wagons. Those of us left behind felt very sad, as we had lost most of our friends. Despite the circumstances we had been like one big family.

Upon arrival in Auschwitz all the children, with the people accompanying them, were sent to the gas chambers. There were no known survivors.

CHAPTER NINETEEN: BERGEN-BELSEN, GERMANY

Exchange Camp

> Buchenwald: a beech wood, a soft word shining with sunlight
> falling through yellow leaves. A name, a place of terror. Ravensbrück:
> bridge of the ravens, a word out of the medieval gloom. Dachau,
> Auschwitz: words with no, so far as I know, particular root meanings,
> but words that leave us confounded and inconsolable. And Bergen-
> Belsen. The name whines like a missile or jet engine. It is a name from
> which there is no escape. And it is impossible to imagine what
> happened at Belsen.
> —"Erica," *Erika: Poems of the Holocaust*, William Heyen

After November 16, 1943, there was a short pause in deportations to the east. No transports left until January 11, 1944, when the first transport from Westerbork went to Bergen-Belsen. After eight months in Westerbork, Edith and I were placed on this transport. While we were walking towards the train, we saw *Kommandant* Gemmeker standing there. Usually he came only when the transports were about to depart. This time he was standing there from the beginning, telling everybody who walked past him, "You people are lucky. You are going to an exchange camp in Germany called Bergen-Belsen." We noticed that the train was not the usual boxcars or cattle wagons but a regular, if very old, passenger train.

We arrived at the railroad station of Bergen early in the morning. I was almost twelve years old. SS guards, yelling and screaming, stood on the platform to receive us. They stood

86

shoulder to shoulder holding big dogs. Yet I don't think anybody dreamed of escaping; we knew that we were in the middle of Germany, somewhere between Hanover and Hamburg. Even though Westerbork was not a concentration camp, food had been sparse, and we looked pale and thin—sickly. I am sure the local population would not have been friendly to anybody trying to escape.

We had to walk to the camp, several kilometers away, under the watchful eyes of the armed SS guards who threatened us with their rifles. This frightened me and I am sure also the other children from the train. The parents tried to comfort some of the smaller children who were crying. Some of the young men and women also tried very hard to comfort the children, especially my sister and me because we were without parents.

We were made to stand for roll call several hours, awaiting our assignment to the barracks. All the time there was the sound of rifle fire in the background, seemingly coming from one of the many watchtowers around the camp. I was very concerned that they were aiming at us and maybe wanting to shoot some or all of us. After a while, we found out that they were not firing directly at us; they were shooting to scare us. This was our reception at Bergen-Belsen and it caused me nightmares for many weeks later.

Our segment of the camp was called the exchange camp by the Germans, but *Sternlager*, or Star Camp, by the rest of the inmates. In the *Sternlager*, we wore our own clothing, by then more like rags, with the Jewish star sewn on. Most other inmates wore the striped prisoner clothing. The conditions in Bergen-Belsen were much harsher than in Westerbork; we got little food—starvation rations. The sanitary conditions were terrible, almost non-existent—a small washroom by each barrack with little water. There were no showers in our segment of the camp. In order to take a shower, the guards had to take us to a different part of the camp. They did not like to do this, so in my sixteen months in Bergen-Belsen I was able to take only two showers. Everybody in the camp was in the same situation. Because of this we were very soon filthy, smelly, and covered in lice, as the straw in the bunks was lice infested.

There were children in the camp, quite a lot of children. We did not know that this situation was unique, that in most other camps there were no children because most children were sent to the death camps, where they were gassed immediately. Moreover, men and women were in the same camp, separated, in different barracks, but husband, wife and children could often meet in the evening— a huge privilege.

In February of 1944, the Birnbaums and the few other children remaining at the orphanage arrived in Bergen-Belsen. Hannah Gosler and her little sister Gabi, then four years old, came with them. I had first met Hannah at the orphanage in Westerbork where she had occupied a bunk right next to my sister Edith and the two had become very friendly.

By the fall of 1944, the first transports arrived from the east because the Germans were evacuating the eastern camps as the Soviet army advanced across Poland. Several transports of women, about 8000 from Auschwitz-Birkenau, arrived at the end of October or the beginning of November. They were put into tents next to us. However, the tents collapsed because of the strong autumn winds. Therefore, half our barracks was taken away to accommodate them. Barbed wire was put up to separate us—straw was stuffed in between so we could not see them. We were forbidden to talk with them.

As I found out years later from my friend, Hannah, or Hanneli, as she was known in Anne Frank's Diary, *her friend, Anne Frank, and Anne's sister, Margot, were among those women. I never knew that Hannah had been Anne Frank's close friend and had lived close to her in Amsterdam. I also did not know at the time that Hannah had talked with Anne several times in Bergen-Belsen.*

Hannah had been surprised and shocked when she found Anne and Margot among the women who had arrived from Auschwitz-Birkenau. She had been under the impression that Anne and her family were safely in Switzerland, a rumor circulated by the Franks when they had gone into hiding in the Annex.

I never knew Anne Frank, but I did read her Diary *after the war*, in 1947, while living in England, a short time after it was published in its original language, Dutch.

Friends in Holland had sent it to me. Not until many years later, in 1989, after seeing a documentary, The Last Seven Months of Anne Frank *by Willy Lindwer, in which Hannah appeared, did I realize that "Hanneli" or "Lies," in* Anne Frank's Diary, *was my sister's and my friend—Hannah Pick Goslar.*

I spent sixteen months in that place, a hell on earth, especially after SS *Kommandant* Joseph Kramer arrived from Auschwitz-Birkenau in the late fall of 1944. Kramer became known as the "Beast of Belsen"; he was notorious for his cruelty. After his arrival, Bergen-Belsen became a concentration camp, and conditions became much, much worse because of the lack of food, water, and medicine. Moreover, the camp became severely overcrowded, increasing from 15,000 to 50,000 or 60,000.

It is still difficult for me to comprehend what happened, how it was possible that people could be so cruel and utterly inhumane, to allow tens of thousands of people to die of starvation and disease, cooped up behind barber wire, living under the most terrible conditions.

Transport 222

To many, in its beak, no dove brought answer.
—"Memento," Stephen Spender

Unlike most of us, a few people at Bergen-Belsen Exchange Camp were finally exchanged. When we were transported to the "exchange camp," we went with a group of people who were part of a Zionist Youth Movement that had been on *hachshara*, or training for life on a *kibbutz*, or collective farm, in preparation to immigrate to Palestine. All of them had actually received immigration certificates from the British Government, allowing them to immigrate to Palestine. However, these certificates arrived after the war started, so they were unable to utilize them. The Germans believed that these certificates had some value to them and, therefore, planned to use the people who had them as exchanges for German citizens interned by the Allies or for German prisoners of war. We did not have Palestine certificates, but because our mother was living in England, we were also considered part of a possible exchange.

The certificate Jews, as they were called, tried very hard to keep up everybody's morale. They were mostly young people in their early twenties who helped each other and also tried to help the rest of us, under very difficult circumstances. I remember well that during the first few months in Bergen-Belsen, many of them, men and women from their separate barracks, would gather in the evening, despite a hard and difficult day, and sing Hebrew songs conducted by their *Madrich* or leader. The German guards were not very happy about this, especially as they were singing forbidden Hebrew songs. They separated the leader from the rest of the group, putting him in a different part of the camp. But I remember that they went defiantly to the barbed wire fence in the evening and sang their songs, while the leader conducted them from the distance.

In the spring and early summer more transports arrived in the *Sternlager*, mainly from Westerbork, but also from other parts, including a transport of Jews from Libya. Although some of the Palestine certificate people were concerned about my sister and me, I saw less of them because a few of my friends from the orphanage in Westerbork had come on one of the transports. Moreover, conditions deteriorated. I don't know if and when they stopped singing or if their leader was able to rejoin them.

In July or August of 1944, I don't remember the exact date, we were suddenly called to a special roll call. I do remember it was a bright sunny day. One of the guards came with a list and started to call out names. The people whose names were called had to prepare themselves, take their meager belongings, and be ready to leave the camp within a few hours. These were the Certificate Jews, and rumor had it that they were to be exchanged for German Nationals held by the British and sent to Palestine. Soon they left, men, women, and children, 222 inmates of the *Sternlager*. Most likely all the *Hachshara* people, who had come with me on the train from Westerbork, were among those to be exchanged except those who were too sick to travel. Again, I don't know whether their leader was among them or even whether he ever returned to our camp.

They were to be exchanged for German Templars, a religious sect that lived in Palestine. In 1939, at the beginning of World War II, the Templars had been interned by the British as enemy aliens. Suddenly in the summer of 1944 the German government wanted them exchanged.

Many months later we did hear rumors that they had arrived in Palestine. Only after the war did we find out that they were first taken to a special part of the camp in order to take showers, clean up, and receive some decent food. They were then taken on a regular passenger train, under the auspices of the International Red Cross and without the SS Guards, across Europe towards Turkey, where the exchange took place. While they were traveling across Yugoslavia a wagon of heavily armed battle ready German soldiers accompanied them to "protect" them from Tito's partisans. Many years later I did meet some people who had been on that train, called Transport 222. They had arrived safely in Palestine.[8]

This was the only real exchange ever to take place from the Bergen-Belsen Exchange Camp. There were some rumors and some names were called later, but nothing after Transport 222 ever materialized.

CHAPTER TWENTY-ONE: BERGEN-BELSEN

Kapos

Instead of mother's milk,
Panic suckles these little ones.
  —"O the Night of the Weeping Children!" Nelly Sachs

It was early morning August 1944. We had to get up in time to be ready for the daily morning roll call. As usual I was tired and hungry. Suddenly I noticed that the routine was somewhat different. Instead of the usual Greek Jewish camp "police" who came around to make sure everybody was up and ready for roll call, a man I had known in Westerbork came around yelling, "Everybody get ready." When I got out of the barrack, I noticed people mingling with one another instead of standing in lines, ready and waiting to be counted at the *Appelplatz*, roll call area.

Something was happening but I didn't know what. I was frightened and thought about sneaking back into the barracks. I did notice that Jacques Albala, the Greek Jewish *Lager Ältester*, or camp leader, and all his Greek Jewish camp police were not present. Ever since our arrival in Bergen-Belsen in January, the group of Greek Jews from Salonika, who had arrived before us, had been in charge of everything, including distributing what little food there was. Unfortunately they were corrupt, stealing food that was supposed to be ours. Now all of a sudden they were gone. The strange thing was that while everybody else was starving and emaciated, Albala was gaining weight. When you entered the Greek barracks in Bergen-Belsen, you thought you had entered another world. I remember the room being warm and cozy. I think too that husbands and wives were together, so the barrack was divided into smaller sections. The biggest difference is that they had more food, especially bread that I hungered for.

Then one of the camp leaders I knew from Westerbork told us that the German SS *Kommandant* had suddenly decided to get rid of Jacques Albala and the Greek camp administration. Even he did not like their corruption. Some German SS guards arrived on the *Appelplatz* together with some strange looking men wearing armbands and signs on their backs, identifying their German titles: "Head *Kapo*," "Runner," "Hospital Orderly," "Food distributor," "Translator," and so forth.

There was a lot of shouting and screaming and we were told to stand in lines to be counted. This was my first introduction to *Kapos*. They spoke very poor German and no Dutch but they knew how to scream. After the usual meaningless head count, the SS left, leaving the *Kapos* in charge. Most of these "new" *Kapos* were not Jews, but Polish prisoners, criminals whom the SS felt they could trust. However, as it turned out, many of them, especially Hank, the head *Kapo*, seemed to be concerned about the conditions in the camp, especially for the children. Our barrack leader, who together with the other barrack leaders had met with the *Kapos*, explained that they had never before seen children in a concentration camp. We were starving, sick, very dirty, and covered with sores and lice. We were also very frightened, wondering what would happen next.

After Albala's dismissal, aside from the *Kapos* who were in charge, a new Jewish *Lager Ältester*, or camp leader, Joseph

Weiss, was appointed from among our camp inmates. He had arrived with us in Bergen-Belsen from Westerbork. Joseph Weiss, whom I happened to know, was, like Hank, very concerned about the children, but there was very little either of them could do. We urgently needed food and medical attention, but that was not available. On this particular day, when I got back to the barrack, I found that Jacques Albala and his family were hiding with us. The SS guards were reluctant to enter our barracks for fear of catching typhus, so most of the Greek camp administration hid in various barracks. Despite their lack of concern about us when they were in charge, we risked hiding them for quite some time. When the SS lost interest in them, they disappeared elsewhere, probably back to their own barracks. In the big mess that was Bergen-Belsen I don't really know what happened to them.[9]

At the end of the day, I had some hope that with the new *Kapos* things might improve in Bergen-Belsen. Unfortunately, they did not.

CHAPTER TWENTY-TWO: BERGEN-BELSEN, GERMANY

Is There a God?

But he bequeathed that hour to his offspring.
They are born with a knife in their hearts.
—"Heritage," Hayim Gouri

I shall never forget late fall and winter of 1944 and 1945. By then, the situation in the *Sternlager* was desperate. We were starving, and typhus was spreading rapidly because of the crowded conditions and the lice. People were dying by the hundreds—and then thousands—of starvation and typhus. The crematorium, partially damaged by an Allied air raid, was overwhelmed. Bodies were left lying all over the camp, stacked up high in front of the barracks, especially in that part of the camp next to ours. So many bodies were piled up there that I was afraid everybody had died. To me, these bodies did not even look like human beings anymore.

Everywhere was the smell of rotting flesh, of death. Some pits were dug and an attempt was made to burn the bodies. The smoke and stench was awful. It must have smelled and been visible for miles around. It is difficult to remember much else about those last few months; we were starving and most of the time could think only of food—and the smell of death.

By March 1945, it seemed as if I had been in this place forever. Early one spring morning, I got up from my bunk to go outside to get some fresh air. The smell inside the barrack was putrid. Once outside, it was not really any better because the dead in the open pits and those piled high by the barracks were being burned. Thick black smoke was in the air—the smell of burning, rotting bodies.

I felt as if I had not eaten for weeks; I was almost beyond hunger. Our rations were down to one thick slice of bread a week and some frozen turnip soup each day. I did not remember when I had last washed or taken a shower. What little water we had was used for drinking.

Some years later, I found out that the International Red Cross had been sending parcels to our camp because we were supposed to be an exchange camp and were considered foreign nationals. Except for one occasion in October 1944, we never received any of those parcels. They were discovered by Allied soldiers, at the end of the war, stacked in several warehouses. The evil and warped Nazis did not give us those parcels, which might have made a difference. More people might have survived this horror.

Every morning, since our arrival in Bergen-Belsen, a group of men and boys would get together and pray the *Shacharit*, or Jewish Morning Prayer, led by one of the rabbis in our camp. At the beginning, I would sometimes participate even though I was not counted as part of the *Minyan*, or ten adult men, as I was not yet thirteen years. I had not gone to this prayer meeting for some time, but this morning I noticed them standing outside the barracks and among them I saw my friend, Josef Holstein, already thirteen, who felt that it was now his duty to assume the responsibilities of an adult. I walked up to him and asked him, "What are you doing?" He answered, "You know what we are doing. This is the *Shacharit*, and you know we do this every morning."

I looked around at all that misery and all the dead, and I asked myself, "My God, to whom and for what are they praying? Then I said, "Maybe we should be saying *Kaddish*" (the Jewish prayer for the dead). Josef never answered me but continued his silent prayers.[10]

Later that afternoon we heard some faint thunder in the distance. One of the Kapos told us that according to some German guards, this was not thunder, but the guns of the Allied army; however, they were still a long way from Bergen-Belsen. Perhaps this morning's prayers had been answered after all? But then the days went by and nothing happened and more people died.

For a while we no longer heard the guns; they were silent.

The Guard

We, the rescued,
From whose hollow bones death had begun to whittle his flutes
—"Chorus of the Rescued," Nelly Sachs

April 1945. In Bergen-Belsen, for some days, we had again been hearing the sounds of gunfire in the distance. Planes flew overhead, constantly bombing, most likely either Hanover or Hamburg. Suddenly, early in the morning on either April 6 or 7, there was a noise in the barracks. Our sector of Belsen, the *Sternlager,* was to be evacuated to the east. The barracks leader called out our names and told us to get ready immediately. About an hour later, under the guard of German soldiers, we walked out of camp with our few belongings. We were a ragged group with tattered clothes, damaged even more when we pulled off the Jewish Star that we had worn all those years. The Germans did not want the local population to know who we were. Many people were almost barefoot, as we no longer had decent shoes.

We walked unnoticed through the town of Bergen; the

inhabitants in the houses on both sides of the road had their shutters closed. Some people in our column fell and were left by the wayside. Then suddenly a small girl fell, and a German guard hurriedly picked her up and helped her to move on. I noticed the guard was crying. I had never before noticed any German guard having sympathy for the children in the camp even though many children were starving to death or dying of typhus. So why was this German guard crying? Did he suddenly take pity on this young girl, or was he upset when he realized it was "all over" and Germany was going to lose the war?

After a long and difficult walk, we finally reached the train station, where a train consisting of many cattle wagons was waiting for us. The floors were covered with straw and it was difficult for most of us, especially the children, to climb into the wagons. Each wagon was very crowded, and we had only a slice of bread each—taken from the camp. Very soon the doors were closed and it became quite dark, as there were no windows, merely a small opening near the top. Then the train began moving, traveling slowly eastward or so some of the people with us seemed to think when they looked out the opening at the top.

This journey continued for about five days. The train stopped many times to let other trains pass and we were even bombed by the Allies a couple of times. Luckily the bombs missed us, but I remember one particularly heavy bombardment near the town of Stendhal. Unfortunately the bombs were not the only danger. Many people died on the way, either of typhus or starvation. On the sixth day, in the morning, the train finally stopped in a small valley or gulch. The guards opened the doors. I had deliberately not spoken German for a number of years, only Dutch, but I asked a German guard what was happening. He answered that they thought a unit of the American Army was in the area and that the engineer had gone to check it out. The guard said, "If the engineer does not return by 11 o'clock, we will leave." Soon after this, they left, but not before offering us the huge amount of bread they had with them. It was mostly dry and moldy but to us it was wonderful. I had not seen so much bread for a long time. But I could not really eat because I was very sick.

Very soon, slowly coming over the hill, the first American soldiers appeared. We had never seen these uniforms before and were not sure who they were. The soldiers also were not sure who we were, but I suspect for a different reason. We must have looked terrifying, like nightmare figures, monsters from something out of science fiction, apparitions arisen from the grave.

They obviously had never seen inmates from concentration camps. At first they would not come near us; they seemed afraid of the prisoners they had come to liberate that April day, in 1945, the thirteenth of April, one week before my thirteenth birthday, near the town of Magdeburg, by the river Elbe.

PART IV

Liberation,
April 1945 - November 1945

How and with what will you fill
Your goblet on the day of Liberation?
—"How?" Abraham Sutzkever

You must not say that you now walk the final way,
Because the darkened heavens hide the blue of day.
The time we've longed for will at last draw near.
And our steps, as drums, will sound that we are here.
—"Zog Nit Keinmol," "Song of the Partisans"

CHAPTER TWENTY-FOUR: LIBERATION

The American Soldier

The stars will remember the gold
the sun will remember the shoes,
the moon will remember the skin.
But who killed the Jews?
                    —"Riddle," William Heyen

April 13, 1945. This small group of soldiers that had appeared on top of the rise, surveyed the train and the strange creatures milling around it. When they came closer, we realized they were not German soldiers, but Americans. They had never been briefed about the possibility of meeting survivors from a concentration camp, what to expect, except maybe that survivors could be infected with typhus, a very dangerous disease. So after a couple of the soldiers ran by the train with their rifles ready to check for enemy soldiers, they withdrew and looked at us from a distance. Because they saw children among the people from the train, they decided maybe those children would like some chocolate. Of course we had not seen chocolate for years; however, as we were all near starvation, it was not what was needed at the moment. It took a little while for us to realize that this was our liberation. Our agony was over. Yet there was very little cheering; people were too sick and exhausted.

The Americans were frontline soldiers and carried few rations with them. So after a while some of the people from the train started to walk to a nearby village, to request some food from the local inhabitants. I was hungry and thirsty. I really wanted some bread and clean water to drink so I decided to head in that same direction. I was feverish and very weak and it took me a long time to reach the village. When I arrived there, the streets were empty; I did not see anybody. I knocked on some doors but nobody answered, until finally I knocked on the front door of a house and a lady appeared to ask me what I wanted. She looked at me in disgust and when I asked for some bread, she told me they had nothing because they were refugees themselves.

Then I sat down on the front steps of the house because I was tired and exhausted. Suddenly a group of soldiers advanced towards me. Now I knew that they were Americans because I had seen similar looking soldiers earlier in the day at the train. They stopped in front of me and started to ask me questions in English but I did not understand a word. I tried to explain to them in German that I had been on a train from a concentration camp and had not eaten anything for several days and that I was looking for food, especially bread. I thought none of the soldiers understood a word of what I was trying to tell them, until one came closer, kneeled down in front of me and asked, "*Du sprichts Yiddish?*" (Do you speak Yiddish?) Even though I did not speak Yiddish, I found out that he understood me and I also understood him, as Yiddish is somewhat similar to German.

He was obviously quite shocked at my appearance; he had tears in his eyes as he questioned me about what I was doing there and where I had came from. He tried to tell the other soldiers about what I had told him. He was very upset and so were the others. They started to take rations from their backpacks to give to me and to take back to the train. The soldier never told me his name, but he decided that I should not have to walk back to the train. Meanwhile, more troops came by and then a column of jeeps appeared. The soldier stopped one of the jeeps, spoke to the driver, and then he helped me to climb on to the back of the jeep, handing me the rations that they had collected for me.

To my surprise, suddenly all the doors of the houses nearby opened and women ran out with their arms loaded with bread and other food and brought it to the jeep for me. The same houses, where nobody answered and where I was told they had nothing because they were also refugees, suddenly had plenty of food to give away. To this very day, I am sure they did this because they saw the American soldiers giving me their rations. They wanted to show that they really cared enough to help a starving Jewish child. I don't think that the Americans knew that they had refused to give me anything before.

The driver of the jeep knew exactly where to take me and when I returned to the train, some of the people told me I was lucky because they had walked to the village, but also had to walk back from the village. No rides for them. I am not sure, but I am fairly certain that somehow I had gone to a different village. I had gone my own way and not paid much attention to where the others were going. I was sick, feverish and, at times, a little delirious. However, because I came back in the jeep with a lot of food, people, including my sister Edith, believed me when I told them about the soldier I had met who had spoken Yiddish.

The next day, the medical officer of the American army unit that had liberated us ordered our evacuation. We were transported in trucks and jeeps to the nearby village of Farsleben and billeted in apartments, which had belonged to German officers who had abandoned those apartments and fled before the arrival of the American army. I was hoping that I would meet the soldier from the previous day again. A lot of soldiers did come to see us because they had heard about the train and its occupants and they wanted to see for themselves what we really looked like. A number of them spoke German quite well, so I could speak to them, but I never again saw "my soldier" who had been so kind to me again. I know he was real and probably I was the first survivor he had ever met. He was shocked because I was so young. But sadly there were still younger children on that train

Maastricht, Netherlands, and Princess Juliana

> We, the rescued,
> Beg you:
> Show us your sun, but gradually
>   Lead us from star to star, step by step.
> Be gentle when you teach us to live again.
>   —"Chorus of the Rescued," Nelly Sachs

After about four weeks, the Americans decided to repatriate us. Because they had nothing else available we were put onto flatbed railroad cars with benches and traveled only by daylight. The first evening the train stopped in a little town (I don't remember the name). We were put up for the night in a huge wooden building, consisting of one very large room or hall, plus some second floor galleries. The building must have been used for large assemblies or gatherings. Because there were no beds or cots, most people slept on the wooden floor. Some people were cooking food on the second floor galleries using small kerosene or oil stoves.

I fell asleep quickly as I was very tired and quite sick. In the middle of the night Edith woke me up. She heard a loud noise and some people were running out of the building. A fire on the upper floor was spreading rapidly. Everybody by now was wide-awake. We all got up, grabbing our few miserable belongings, and ran for the doors. It was quite a crush. Fortunately the building had huge doors in the front and back, so despite the panic, everybody managed to get out of the building without being hurt. Because it was a wooden building, the fire spread rapidly. We stood at a distance, watching the building burn down completely. As far as I remember no fire engine ever came, and as there were no buildings standing close by, there seemed to be no danger of the fire spreading. I guess the local authorities were either afraid of coming near us or did not care if maybe a few Jews returning from a concentration camp were burned.

After watching the building burning to the ground, everybody slowly started walking towards the train, standing in the dark. We really had nowhere else to go. I don't know when we were supposed to leave, but the train started to move before dawn. I imagine the Americans in charge of the train decided there was no point staying in the little town any longer. I knew that nobody was hurt in the fire, but I was never quite sure whether everybody got back on the train. Also I never found out whether the fire was an accident. After all, people were using kerosene stoves on the second floor. However, some people on the train seemed to believe that the fire had been set by a local Nazi or hooligan upset that the war was lost, thinking perhaps that he could kill a few more Jews.

During the day, we passed through several cities—almost totally destroyed, either by bombardment from the air or through battle. Every time we entered one of those cities, some of us on the train, including myself, cheered upon seeing Germany in ruins. We stopped in one of those cities to get some water to drink. The May sun was very hot and we ate some bread. People would gather and look at us from a "safe" distance.

That evening, we stopped for a short while again to refill our water bottles and eat some bread. I am sure other food was available, but many other people, including my sister and I, could not really eat anything else. After the fiasco of the night before, we slept on the train, which started moving at dawn.

After three days we arrived in the Dutch city of Maastricht and by that time I was so ill that I was taken off the train and put into a temporary hospital established in a convent. My sister was also taken off, but put into a different hospital. The train continued to a debriefing center, located in a nearby castle, where the local authorities, with the Americans, tried to help people to put their lives back together, finding out where people came from and where they wanted to go. Most of northern Holland had been liberated only at the end of the war and part of the south had been badly damaged during the big battles that had taken place in the fall and winter of 1944. However, Maastricht was in good shape, as American forces had liberated that city on September 4, 1944, with hardly a shot fired.

The first few days in the hospital I was semi-conscious, but I did notice that early in the morning a priest would come to say prayers. Later on I found out that by some curious coincidence I was the youngest person in the ward and also the only Jew. The rest of the patients were mainly returning Dutch who had worked in the resistance, been caught, and sent to various concentration camps in Germany. The nurses were nuns, who were dedicated and took very good care of me. These gentle sisters fed, bathed, and clothed me. Slowly I started to recuperate. The nuns knew that Jews had been persecuted and deported by the Germans during the war, but they had not understood what had happened until the survivors started to return.

After about two months I had fully recuperated but as I had nowhere to go, the nuns were very concerned what would happen to me next. My sister also was better and we were taken to city hall to register so that there would be a record of our return. The clerk asked us where we had lived in Holland and we told him Dinxperlo. He asked our place of birth and we told him Germany. The next question, "What was our nationality?"

We answered, "Stateless." The clerk then told us, "There is no such thing as stateless, that was the Nazis' law and now that Germany has been defeated, this law is cancelled." He then told us because we were German citizens he would have to send us back to Germany. The nuns would not agree to this, so for a short while we returned to the hospital.

A few days later, there was a visit by Princess Juliana of the Netherlands, the daughter of Queen Wilhelmina and heiress to the throne. She came to visit all the returning Dutch who had suffered in the concentration and slave labor camps. The men in my ward decided I should come with them. It was a beautiful early summer day and we were assembled in the courtyard of city hall to receive the princess. She came and tried to shake hands and greet as many people as possible. When she came to us, one of the men with me spoke to her about the plight of my sister and me. She listened intently, then shook my hand, and moved on. A few days later we were taken out of the hospital and housed temporarily in a local school together with children of collaborators, whose parents had been put into prison camps.

We learned then that German Jewish refugees who had come to The Netherlands after *Kristallnacht* and had survived concentration or death camps were put into those prison camps upon their return together with collaborators. The nuns found this whole situation intolerable. Because of their insistence, we only slept at the school and were free to go where we wanted during the day. They tried to find a solution and after a few days they were informed that Mr. Birnbaum and his wife, who had run the orphanage in Westerbork and survived Bergen-Belsen, were in Maastricht on their way to Laren near Amsterdam where a Jewish orphanage had been established. They asked us whether we would like to go with them and we agreed because we knew the Birnbaums from Westerbork and had spent some time in the orphanage. The nuns were very pleased, even though they continued to be concerned about our fate. About this time, at the insistence of Princess Juliana, the Dutch government agreed that all the German Jewish refugees who had arrived in Holland before the war and had survived could stay in Holland—as long as was necessary for them to reorganize their lives. I like to believe that I was partially responsible for this happening.

We were then taken to the orphanage at Laren by American army trucks. The roads were still in very bad shape from the bombings and shellings, so it took about twelve hours before we arrived there. On the way, we stopped in Amsterdam for a short while. We were allowed to get out of the trucks and people living in the area came to "check us out," as word got out that we were children who had survived a concentration camp.

After only three days at the orphanage, we were asked to come to the office. There we met our Uncle Adolf, who had been in hiding ever since the German invasion of May 10, 1940. Aunt Martha and cousin Margot had joined him later and together they had survived. They were the only ones of our family who lived in Holland to survive the war. He had been looking for us for several weeks because our names had been on a list published by the Dutch Red Cross of Jews from Holland who had survived the various death and concentration camps. However, there had been no indication of where we were staying. He had finally gone to Maastricht, arriving there a day after we left. The nuns told him where to find us.

We were elated to see our uncle. He, Aunt Martha, and Margot were living in Utrecht, so we immediately went with him to stay at their house. We arrived in Utrecht in July 1945.

Utrecht, Netherlands

Nation shall not lift up sword against nation,
Neither shall men learn war anymore,
For all men, both great and small, shall know the Lord.
　　　　　　—Isaiah 2.4

After our arrival in Utrecht, my uncle and aunt decided I should start going to school. Yet I had not been to school for over two years. I was, therefore, somewhat apprehensive; I thought that I would be way behind all the other children. On the first day in school, I was told by the head mistress, "Don't worry! You will be fine." Because I was thirteen years old I was put in the eighth grade. This school, called Puntenburg, had been closed the last few months of the war, as were most schools in Utrecht. So even though it was summer, they all were in session, making up for the time they had been closed.

I felt uncomfortable in school; I was not used to it anymore. I tried very hard to comprehend everything, but I somehow had the feeling I was failing. I complained to my uncle and aunt, who then sent my cousin Margot, to speak to the headmistress of the school. The head mistress told Margot, "He should not worry so much. He is doing fine and will soon catch up to the rest of the children."

Slowly, I started to get used to the idea of going to school regularly and even began to enjoy it, especially meeting other children and making new friends. I told them very little about my experiences in the camps, but they told me that during the last few months of the war, in the spring of 1945, the northwestern part of Holland, including the major cities such as Amsterdam, The Hague, Rotterdam, and Utrecht had been isolated from the rest of the country and they had very little food. Especially in the cities people had been starving. Consequently many people had gone into the countryside to try to buy a little food from the local farmers, who did not have much either. This was one of the reasons the schools had been closed.

My uncle now decided I should have a *bar mitzvah,* the Jewish tradition of coming of age at age thirteen. My *bar mitzvah* should have been in April, but of course that had been impossible. The rabbi of the local synagogue, Rabbi Van Gelderen, who had survived the war, suggested a date sometime in late September in order for me to have enough time to learn to read from the *Torah.* I went to Rabbi Van Gelderen's house, next to the synagogue, nearly every day after school to study. I became very friendly with his two children, a girl who was about my age and a boy, a few years older. I think the girl's name was Jupie, but I cannot remember the boy's name. Their presence and encouragement meant a lot to me.

The *bar mitzvah* itself was great. Utrecht used to have a fairly large Jewish population before the war, but most did not return. The question was, Would there be enough men for a *minyan,* or quorum, on the Sabbath of my *bar mitzvah?* However, word had gone out to the Canadian soldiers, at the time occupying that part of Holland, about the first *bar mitzvah* to be held at the synagogue in Utrecht since the war. So on the day of the *bar mitzvah* there was almost an "overflow" crowd in the synagogue, mostly Canadian soldiers. Probably some of them were not Jewish, but that did not matter.

I had invited my friend Josef Holstein who was at the time in an orphanage not too far away (see Bergen-Belsen: Chapter 22). Josef was very happy to be a part of the festivities. He read or chanted the *Haftarah* from the *Book of the Prophets* at the conclusion of the *Torah* service. Originally my uncle wanted to do this part, but when he noticed that Josef very much wanted to chant the *Haftarah*, he felt it was the right thing to do on this occasion.

Later Rabbi Van Gelderen and his family immigrated to Israel. There was really no Jewish community left in Utrecht. The synagogue was sold and eventually became a church.

My *bar mitzvah* was the highlight of our stay in Utrecht.

In the meantime, Uncle Adolf had been in touch with our mother in England, telling her that he had been looking for us. Now that he finally found us, our mother started to make arrangements for us to come to England. A short time later, in November 1945, we were finally able to join our mother.

Physical Map of the World, June 2003

PART V

After the Shoah, 1945-98

For I am a stranger with thee, and a sojourner,
as all my fathers were.
—Psalms, 39:12

Each generation must create its own humanity.
—"If," Edward Bond

CHAPTER TWENTY-SEVEN: AFTER THE SHOAH

England

For Mercy has a human heart.
—"The Divine Image," William Blake

I arrived in England in November 1945, and reunited with my mother after not having seen her for almost six years. We had traveled overnight by ship from Hoek van Holland, a small port near Rotterdam, Holland, to Harwich in England. Before the war, this had been the quickest and most popular route from Holland to England. My mother had taken the last passenger ship from Hoek van Holland on September 1, 1939 before the war started. This route had been reopened only a few days earlier—after all the mines had been cleared. Apparently we were on the first passenger ship on this route since the end of the war. We were together with eight other young Jewish children who had survived the war in Holland and who, like Edith and I, were on their way to England to join parents or relatives.

The Canadian army that had liberated most of Holland and worked very hard at restoring normal civilian life facilitated this trip. They were anxious to reunite children with parents or relatives. They took us by army truck from Amsterdam to Hoek van Holland accompanied by some soldiers to take us to the ship. Railways were not yet functioning properly in Holland and most passenger trains had been destroyed. A Canadian WAC (Women's Army Corps) had the task of accompanying us to England. Upon arrival in Harwich, we went through a lot of formalities before we were allowed to board the train to London, where our mother would be waiting for us.

I was apprehensive; I had not seen my mother for over six years. A lot had happened and I did not know quite how to react. In fact, I did not really remember my mother that well. After the war, I had been very comfortable living with my Uncle Adolf in Utrecht, Holland, and I would have been quite happy to stay there. But I knew that I had to go to England to be with my mother who had suffered immensely during those years—not knowing what had happened to us. After about a two-hour train ride, we finally arrived in London.

I immediately recognized my mother standing on the platform. There was a lot of excitement anyway because all the other kids had their parents or relatives waiting for them. We ran to our mother and I noticed she was crying, but these were tears of happiness and relief because she saw that we looked well and we had of course grown a lot since the last time she had seen us. My sister also cried and then I started to cry because everybody else was crying and that somehow affected me. We had a lot to talk about and we still had a long train ride to Leeds, where my mother was living. The Canadian WAC gave my mother all the paper work, wishing us much good luck and happiness.

Most of the other kids were staying in London, but we took a taxi to another train station for the train to Leeds, a journey of about four hours. We talked quite a lot, but my sister did most of the talking. I was very excited about being in a new country and the train ride fascinated me; I was not used to the fact that passenger trains could be clean, have seats, and function normally. Towards evening, when it was already dark, we arrived in Leeds and the start of a new life for me.

To me England was a strange country. I understood neither the language nor the customs. My mother wanted me to go to school almost immediately, but I was reluctant as I had not been to school for nearly three years, except for the few months in Utrecht, Holland.

My mother hired a private tutor so that it would be easier and quicker for me to learn English. After two months I finally went to school, to the ninth grade. The first few days were hectic. I had to change my name from Fritz to Fred, as German names were not too popular in England at that time. I was a curiosity to the other children. I spoke English with a strange accent and when things became difficult I lapsed into Dutch. To my surprise I noticed that except for the language I was not that far behind. After a few weeks I was promoted to a different class, for very bright students. The teacher, Mr. Flatley, was very interested in me because he had been a paratrooper during the war and had parachuted into Holland in 1944 during the battle for Walcheren, a strategic island in the south of Holland.

I think in order to make me feel comfortable with my English, Mr. Flatley gave me letters he had received from friends in Holland to translate. I always remember this teacher because I think he understood my problems and during history and world affairs lessons he always mentioned how much the Dutch and especially the Jews had suffered during the recent war. He said they should believe him, for after all he had been there and witnessed some of it. He would then point to me and say, "If you need to verify what I just told you, please ask Fred because he was there during those years."

In those days in England in order to go to "grammar school" or high school you had to pass a special test at age eleven. This test was quite difficult, so usually only top students or the children of the wealthy who had private tuition could pass that test. Because I came to England at age thirteen and a half, I could not take that test, and they were not willing to make an exception, even though I felt my circumstances warranted such an exception. So I went to school in what was called then a "secondary modern school," good only until the age of fifteen.

After that I was on my own. I received some more private tuition and by that time, I had joined a Zionist Youth Movement, *Hashomer Hatzair*, which emphasized education; we were challenged to read a lot and educate ourselves. We had many seminars, workshops, and discussion groups in order to further our education.

My mother realized that I could not go back to being a child, even though I was not yet fourteen years old when I arrived in England. She tried hard to adjust to the fact that during seven years of my life between the ages of six and thirteen, I had not lived with her and that most of those years had been terrible. I had grown up much too early. I had lost my childhood. The adjustment was difficult for both of us. Yet she let me more or less make my own decisions. She would make suggestions, if she were not happy with what I was doing. The problem was that I was restless. She was not happy that I was planning to go to Israel.

In 1949 at the age of seventeen I went to *Hachshara*, in preparation for life on a *kibbutz*, or collective farm in Israel. In those days this was still a common thing to do if you were in a Zionist Youth movement and wanted to make *Aliyah*, or immigrate to Israel. I really wanted to go to Israel in 1948 during the War of Independence, but I was told that I was too young. On *Hachshara*, among other things, we learned to become farmers and live on a *kibbutz*. But we also continued with our education; the *Hachshara* was like going to a "working college."

At this time, I received notification to report for the examination for conscription (the draft). In those days England still had conscription; every young man at the age of eighteen had to register and then go for tests in order to decide what branch of the army he would join. Some of my friends who did not want to join the British army decided that their time had come to immigrate to Israel. However, some of us needed to remain behind for the time being in order to keep the farm going. I was among those staying behind, for I had health problems because of the time I had spent in Bergen-Belsen. I felt the army would reject me because of these health problems. But in order to play it safe I registered for the Royal Air Force, so in case I was accepted I would at least learn something.

On the day that I went for the physical, I first had to go through a mental evaluation. I thought this test was very easy— multiple choice—and I completed the test in half the time allotted with a one hundred percent score. After I finished I noticed many of the group of young men who were doing the same test struggling to find the answers. Some of them were a few years older and had graduated college and yet could not answer those questions. At the time I found it very strange to see most of those young men struggling to answer fairly routine questions, especially college graduates.

The officer in charge came over to me, just to make sure that I really had answered everything. He then wanted me to sign on for several years, saying that the Royal Air Force was looking for people like me. I told him, "I may not pass the physical." At the physical examination there were eight different doctors. However, the doctor who made the final decision had been in the British army that had liberated Bergen-Belsen. After hearing that I had spent almost sixteen months in that camp, he felt that I was not fit, physically, to serve in either the Royal Air Force or the army.

So I did not go into the British army. I spent several more years on *Hachshara* and I helped them to move the location from Bedford in the south of England to Bishop's Stortford, a rural area, not too far from London. In November 1952 I finally immigrated to Israel.

The Wandering Jew

From lands all white with snow to land all green with palms.
—paraphrase, *"Zog Nit Keinmol,"* "Song of the Partisans"

I arrived in Israel in December 1952. I first lived in *Kibbutz Ein Hachoresh,* in central Israel before moving to Kibbutz Zikim in the south right by the border with Gaza. Zikim was a young *kibbutz* and it desperately needed help, especially with the many problems facing a border kibbutz trying to farm the land in those days. We would work by day and stand guard by night as infiltrators from the Gaza Strip constantly threatened us.

In 1954 I was drafted into the army, a special unit called *Nachal,* which after basic training was sent to border settlements to protect them. We were sent to *Kibbutz Yad Mordechai,* near the border with Gaza.[11] There were nightly infiltrations across the border and our job was to stop them. During the 1956 Suez War I was still in the army, and for the first time I saw the Sinai desert and the Suez Canal, which had been closed by the Egyptians.

Shortly after, in 1957, I was released from the army and went back to *Kibbutz Zikim.* In the fall of 1958 I went to visit some friends in England, and from there I took a ship bound for Valparaiso, Chile. My mother and Edith had moved to Chile, after I had left for Israel, and I was planning to visit them.

The four-week trip by ship was a "cruise like" voyage. We stopped in many ports including Havana, Cuba, just a few weeks before Fidel Castro came to Havana. We also passed through the Panama Canal. I met a number of interesting young people including two German girls, sisters, Ilse and Edith, who were accompanying the British Ambassador to Panama, traveling first class, to take care of his young children. Both were young, twenty and twenty two, and when they found out who I was, they insisted on accompanying me every time we went ashore at the various ports. Because I was traveling tourist class that was usually the only time I could see them, except when they managed to sneak into the tourist section some evenings, with the help of the Chief Purser, a young man who also came along when we went ashore.

I found out that their father had been in an SS unit in Russia and had been a prisoner of war, only returning home in 1954. The older girl Ilse flirted with the idea of marrying me. Aside from the fact that I was not yet ready to marry, I certainly was not going to marry a German girl, especially the daughter of an ex SS officer. I never told her that; I just said I am not ready to marry. I could not imagine after arriving in Chile, telling my mother and my relatives, "I am going to marry a German girl, the daughter of a SS officer."

My visit to Chile lasted about five years. I learned Spanish and worked for some time for *Italmar*, the Italian Line and a passenger shipping company. So I also learned some Italian. However, even though I had a lot of family in Chile, I never really liked living there. One of the reasons was the huge difference between wealthy and poor. There was only a small middle class, mainly the immigrants from Europe. About 98% of the population lived in abject poverty. I knew somehow that this situation could not continue much longer. I was even more convinced after meeting once with Salvador Allende from the left wing socialist party, who aspired to be president. Actually about seven years after I left Chile, Allende became president.

I left Chile in 1963. Instead of returning to Israel, I decided to try the United States. I had no problem obtaining an immigrant visa, as in those days visas went according to the quota system and I was under the German quota, which at that time was never filled because of the *Wirtschaftwunder*, the new prosperity in Germany.

I arrived in the United States in October of 1963, and I immediately found work at the Zim lines or the American-Israeli Shipping Company. They were putting a brand new passenger ship, the *Shalom*, into service and they needed some expertise, such as I had learned from the Italian Line while I worked for them in Chile. However, the time of the big transatlantic ocean liners was almost over because airplanes were much quicker, especially in the Jet Age, which was just beginning. The only way to use the ship successfully would be as a cruise ship and the Israeli government, which owned a large part of Zim, was not thrilled because of the *Kashrut*, or kosher problem. After a few years the *Shalom* was sold to a German cruise line and I left Zim in 1967 to work for El Al as their sales manager in New Jersey.

In 1968 I was twice sent to Israel to attend courses at the headquarters of El Al in Lod (Lydda). While in Israel at the end of 1968, I met my future wife Yael, a *Sabra* or Israeli-born. We were married in Israel in December 1969, but we continued to live in the USA. I worked for El Al for almost thirty-two years and I could write a book just about that: I was never bored. At the end of 1998 I decided to retire. I felt I needed a little less excitement. Aside from a part time job as a salesman and consultant for a tour company called Gate 1 of Glenside, Pennsylvania, I have since spent a lot of time at schools and colleges speaking about my experiences during the Shoah

City of Death

"The sun shone, the acacias bloomed, and the slaughterer slaughtered." Thus wrote the Hebrew poet Chaim Nachman Bialik in his poem the "City of Death" after the 1905 Pogrom in Kishenev, Russia. I often wonder what kind of poetry Bialik, who died in 1934, would have written had he lived during the Holocaust. Could he have written any poetry at all about such a disastrous and horrible event? What would he have called Auschwitz or any of the other death camps? Yet somehow this poem is always in my mind when I think about my experiences during those years when the killing was going on in the ghettos and concentration camps all over Europe. Despite this, most people still lived normal lives, watching the sun rise and the acacias bloom.

I often ask myself, How was it possible? Why did it happen in twentieth century Europe, the center of world civilization and culture, the Germany of Goethe, Heine, and Mendelsohn? And why did the rest of the world turn its back and ignore us? Were they so blinded by the sun that they did not see the slaughterer? Or maybe the smell of the acacias blooming hid the smell of death, of burning and rotting bodies.

Excuses abound, and some of them are valid. The powerful German army conquered most of Europe and the Jews were trapped. Yet many could have escaped had the United States not closed its borders to Jewish immigration and the British not prohibited immigration to what in those days was Palestine, today Israel.

There are a few heroic exceptions where people were not blinded and did not turn their backs. These few saw the attempt to destroy an entire people and religion and did their best to help at great risk to themselves. These righteous rescuers should be revered and honored because they recognized the slaughterer and tried to save people. They were not fooled by the blooming of the acacias; they did the right thing—the ethical thing. Unfortunately there were not enough of them to stop the slaughter in the many camps of death and destruction.

I am asked many times by children in schools and colleges when I speak to them about my experiences during those years. "Why did it happen? Could it happen again?" The answer is: The world did not care and that is why it happened. Unfortunately it could happen again because most people still do not care. Witness the many genocides that have occurred since the Holocaust. Also antisemitism is problematic again in Europe of today.

I sometimes wonder, when I tell my story, Is it possible? Did all this really happen? Unfortunately, the answer is yes. It is all long ago, but the memories are real and frightening. These memories of what happened are impossible to suppress. We should not forget because if we do, we are doomed, and the *Shoah* will happen again. Because of this, we have to tell and teach the future generations about what happened, when the sun shone, the acacias bloomed, and the slaughterer slaughtered.

> *Vengeance is [God's] own;*
> *To prove He's not abandoned us*
> *He gave the gift of memory,*
> *The fruit of all the trees*
> *In the Land of Israel.*
>   —*"Synagogue in Prague,"* Alan Sillitoe

Sigmund Spiegel, Fred's father, Dinslaken, Germany, 1913.
The Steinhoff's great-grandfather's brothers are the two men standing
third and fourth from the left.

Sigmund Spiegel, Dinslaken, Germany, 1914.

Fred's mother and father, wedding (left) and honeymoon (right),
Dinslaken, Germany, 1927.

Mother, father, and Edith, Dinslaken, Germany, 1928.

Mother, Essen, 1930s.

Fritz and sister Edith with mother and father, Dinslaken, Germany, 1932.

Fritz and Grandfather Louis Spiegel, Dinslaken, Germany, 1934.

Fritz with mother, friend, Aunt
Martha, and Aunt Erna, Essen, 1935.

Fritz, Gennep, Netherlands, 1940.

Fritz, Gennep, Netherlands, 1940.

Fritz, Dinxperlo, Netherlands, 1942.

Edith, Dinxperlo, Netherlands, 1942.

Fritz on right 2nd row, next to friend Isaac Menist (see memorial photo on page 149), Dinxperlo, Netherlands, 1942.

Sophie Berghausen (maternal grandmother), Edith, Fritz, and Julius Berghausen (maternal grandfather), Enschede, Netherlands, 1942.

Edith, Fred, and mother, Leeds, England, 1946.

Fred and Edith, Leeds, England, 1946.

Fred, Leeds, England, 1947.

Fred before immigrating to Israel, England, 1952.

Mother, Vina del Mar, Chile, 1969.

Fred and Yael wedding, Yokneam,
Israel, December 10, 1969

Memorial to the synagogue at
Dinxperlo, May 1995

Fred, Westerbork, Orphanage
marker, 2000

Willy and Henny, Lieber, Nijmegen, Holland, 2002

Mr. and Mrs. Steinhoff, Fred, Brigitte and Christiane Steinhoff, Dinslaken, 2000. (See football team photo page 129. The two Steinhoffs pictured in that photo are brothers of Brigitte and Christiane's great-grandfather.)

Yuval, Fred, Yael, Nancy, Omri, Avital, at Omri and Nancy's wedding
New Jersey, November 9, 2002

Lisa, Fred, Yvonne, Dinslaken, 2003

Part VI

Commemoration and Reflection

1998 – 2003

I believe in the sun
Though it is late
In rising

I believe in love
Though it is absent

I believe in God
Though he is
Silent . . .

—"I Believe," unsigned inscription in a cave
in Cologne where Jews had been hiding.

Commemorating Westerbork

You who live secure
In your warm houses,
Who return at evening to find
Hot food and friendly faces:

Consider whether this is a man,
Who labours in the mud
Who knows no peace
Who fights for a crust of bread
Who dies at a yes or a no.
Consider whether this is a woman,
Without hair or name
With no more strength to remember
Eyes empty and womb cold
As a frog in winter.

Consider that this has been:
I commend these words to you.
                    —*"Shema,"* Primo Levi

April 12, 2000.   Fifty-five years after I was liberated by American troops from a cattle train near Magdeburg. Fifty-five years since the liberation of transit camp Westerbork in Holland. I had spent eight months in Westerbork as an eleven year-old boy, from May 1943 until January 1944. Now a commemoration.

For years, the Dutch have tried to ignore what happened in Holland during the Second World War. Most of the Jewish population there perished and relatively little was done to help. Only now, after these many years, things seem slowly to be changing. Hopefully the younger generations will come to grips with what their grandparents did or did not do. The commemoration at Westerbork was to be an important event. Survivors from all over the world were invited, and some of us gathered in a motel near the town of Assen north of Westerbork a couple of days before. Nearly all the participants brought their spouses and some came with their children. I had never been north of Westerbork, so everything was new to me. A day before the commemoration, we were offered a tour of "Jewish Groningen." Groningen is a large city about thirty kilometers north of Westerbork.

While waiting in the lobby of the motel, we started to get to know each other. Recognizing the survivors was easy because of their age. We exchanged anecdotes about those days. One of the men I met had actually escaped from Westerbork in 1943, one of the few, as only twenty people managed to escape successfully out of a total of 106,000 Jews who passed through Westerbork.

Groningen had a Jewish population of over 3000 before the war; however, very few survived. An interesting synagogue there has been restored and is being used by the few remaining Jews living in Groningen. Most of them are immigrants from the former Soviet Union. The synagogue is also being used as a social hall for the local population. A local Jewish professor gave us an interesting history of the Jewish population of Groningen. For me it was a revelation because he mentioned the children's book author, Clara Asscher Pinkhof, whom I had met in Westerbork while I was there in 1943. She used to come to the orphanage, where I was, to teach and be with the children. I now learned that she had been the wife of Rabbi Asscher who came to Groningen in 1926 and tried to liberalize the Jewish community. Unfortunately Rabbi Asscher died soon after his arrival in Groningen and left his widow with five children. In order to make a living Clara started to write children's books. She was later sent from Westerbork to Bergen-Belsen to the Star Camp, or *Sternlager*. She was fortunate enough to be part of the only exchange ever taking place from this camp, whereby 222 Jews were exchanged in the summer of 1944 and sent to Palestine in exchange for German Templars, a Christian religious sect that had been living in Palestine, interned by the British in 1939 as enemy aliens. Now they were being repatriated. Asscher Pinkhof wrote the book *Star Children* about her experiences.

The tour of Groningen was very well organized. Aside from the synagogue, we saw one of the oldest railroad stations in Holland, which was being restored; we toured the old city and went to City Hall, which had an exhibition of old paintings of Groningen. The mayor of Groningen gave a special reception. That evening the village of Westerbork invited us for dinner at a local restaurant. This village is located about ten kilometers from the former campsite. Unfortunately, the people at the *Herinneringscentrum* or museum at Westerbork had failed to indicate to the people at the village that most people participating were Jewish. At the very beautiful buffet dinner, most of the hot dishes were pork. That same evening, at the museum, an excellent theater group put on a performance based on the book *Binnen de Poorten* (*Inside the Doors*), written by Jules Schelvis, a survivor of Sobibor. As noted afterward, of 35,000 Jews who were transported from Westerbork to Sobibor in the spring and summer of 1943 only nineteen survived. This was the first time the play was performed, and it was so well done that even those people who did not understand Dutch were able to comprehend most of it.

The next day, April 12, was the day for the commemoration. It was a gray and cool day with a threat of rain, typical Westerbork weather for that time of the year. The ceremony was scheduled for two o'clock in the afternoon. The area where the camp and barracks were located is about five kilometers from the museum. I had arranged to meet some friends at the museum, including two high school girls and their teacher from a high school in Dinslaken, Germany, the town where I was born. Their class was working on a Holocaust project that included the biography of some Jews who had been born in Dinslaken and had survived the Holocaust. As Dinslaken is about two and a half hours drive they decided to come and meet me. This way we would meet beforehand and proceed to the ceremony together, as about three thousand people were expected to attend. They did not arrive in time, so we decided to go in order not to miss part of the ceremony, hoping that we would meet them there.

The event was scheduled to take place by the original, symbolic, very moving memorial, whose centerpiece is a railroad track with the ends pointing upwards to the heavens. Present were a lot of youth who covered the railroad tracks with flowers. The ceremony itself was short but very moving. A few speeches, then the names of the children from Westerbork, who had perished in the Holocaust, were read with the sound of bells ringing in the background. *El Ma'aleh* and *Kaddish* were said, and a bugler sounded "taps."

In the middle of the ceremony there was a tap on my shoulder—the girls (the Steinhoff twins) from Dinslaken had finally arrived with their teacher Gabriele Khanna and Professor Klaus Tofahrn and recognized me from a photo. After everything was over, I explained to them about Westerbork and showed them where some of the barracks had been, including the orphanage, where I had been for seven months. There are no barracks left in Westerbork. Afterwards we went back to visit the museum. The students seemed to be quite impressed by everything. The teacher told me that the whole class was going to visit Israel a few weeks later to stay in their sister city, Arad, and present their Holocaust project to the high school there.

A special meeting had been planned for the survivors and their relatives at the *Provinciehuis* in Assen later in the afternoon and, after saying goodbye to everybody at the museum, I went there together with my wife, Yael.

Assen, the capital of the province of Drente, is the nearest city to Westerbork. We met and talked to a lot of people at this meeting. They even provided kosher sandwiches. We met an orthodox rabbi there, who had been in Westerbork and Bergen-Belsen as a very young child; he had been three years old at the time of his liberation by Russian troops on a train near Trobitz. He did not remember anything; his father had died in the camp and his mother never talked about their experiences. So he was trying to piece together what happened to him by talking to other people. He felt that even though he had been invited to be present at the commemoration, the people at the museum who were in charge of the event really did not know what to do with him or, for that matter, with all of the survivors who had been invited and came from all over the world. This is the same complaint I heard from a survivor who had come all the way from Australia. The whole event was well covered by Dutch TV. Many children and young adults attended, and for me this made it all worthwhile. However, among the over 3000 people attending were at most two hundred survivors, also some relatives, but mostly people who wanted to be at the ceremony and a lot of schoolchildren. So maybe they should have somehow mentioned our presence.

I hope that I will still be able to go to Westerbork for the sixtieth anniversary of the liberation.

CHAPTER THIRTY-ONE: COMMEMORATION

Vught Revisited 2003

The dead have remembered
our indifference
The dead have remembered
our silence
The dead have remembered
our words
　　　　　—"Posthumous Rehabilitation," Tadeusz Rozewicz

I never really wanted to revisit camp Vught. The memories of my first concentration camp were bitter and I had tried as much as possible to forget them. I finally decided to visit the National Monument Camp Vught while in the Netherlands on vacation in 2003. One of the reasons I decided to go was that in the spring of 2002 I had received an email from Joost Seelen, a producer working on a documentary about Vught. He asked me whether there was any chance of my coming to the Netherlands because he would like to interview me about my experiences at that camp. He had read on the Dinxperlo Website my article "A Day in Vught."

I wrote back to him that I would be on vacation in Westduin, near Vlissingen, Zeeland, a resort in the south of the Netherlands, at the beginning of August 2002. I would be happy to meet with him then. The interview was to be taped in Breda, about an hour's drive from Westduin. A car was sent to pick me up, together with my wife Yael. Eric Duivenvoorden did the interview and I think it went well. I had told them beforehand that because my Dutch was not too good anymore, I would prefer that it would be done in English and they had agreed. The documentary was to be viewed on Dutch TV on May 5, 2003.

A few months before the documentary was to be shown, I received word from Joost Seelen that they had decided not to include my interview because mine were the memories of a child. I was somewhat surprised because they had originally been very anxious to include my interview in the documentary.

Because of what happened with the documentary I needed to go and visit Vught to try and understand more fully what had happened to me and the other children there during those awful weeks in the spring of 1943.

We had gone to Vught in 2002, on our way to Westduin, but it was closed for renovation. It reopened in October 2002 with a completely renovated museum.

I was very impressed with the museum. There is a lot of documentation about what happened from January 1943, when the camp opened, until September 1944, when the camp was evacuated because of the advancing allied armies. According to the explanation given at the museum (this is sometimes disputed), Vught was the only SS concentration camp in the Netherlands and the only SS concentration camp outside of Nazi Germany during World War Two. Vught was controlled directly by the SS headquarters in Oranienburg, Germany.

A total of about 31,000 prisoners were in the camp at one time or another, some just for a short while and some longer. Of those more than 12,000 were Jews. For the Jewish inmates of Vught, the camp was a temporary place. As of February 1943, the Jewish segment was called *Judendurchgangslager*, or Jewish transit camp. Some of the families with children had already been transported to Westerbork and on to the death camps in April and May 1943. Very few survived. As you have read, our family, with the exception of Ruth, was put on a transport to

Westerbork on May 23, 1943. Most families on that transport were deported to Sobibor the next day and were murdered. By luck, my cousin Alfred and I escaped that transport. Unfortunately Alfred, Uncle Max, and Aunt Paula were sent to Sobibor about six weeks later and murdered upon their arrival.

By the end of April 1943, about 1800 children were in concentration camp Vught—from birth to age sixteen. Conditions were so harsh that many children became sick and some died. Because the rumor spread outside the camp that the children were very sick and dying of hunger and disease, the SS administration decided to get rid of all the children. On June 6 and 7, 1943, the infamous *kinder* transports were organized, whereby the 1269 children still in Vught were sent to Westerbork together with at least one of their parents or other older family members. Next day, June 8, all were deported to Sobibor and murdered on their arrival. A memorial to those 1269 children was unveiled on September 5, 1999, on the site of the National Monument with the names and ages of these murdered children. There is a photograph of part of the monument in the Museum and by coincidence it shows the names of Isaac and Jetty Menist, my friends from Dinxperlo. The names of the children from those transports had been kept in the archives of Vught.

The last transport of Jews from Vught took place on June 2, 1944, when those working at the Philips factories, 496 people, including my cousin Ruth, were deported directly to Auschwitz. Of those 382 survived the war. Aside from these Philips workers, very few Vught Jews returned from the various death and concentration camps.

All of the facts above are documented at the museum. The date of our transport is documented at the *Nederlands Instituut voor Oorlogsdocumentatie*, Netherlands Institute for War Documentation in Amsterdam. The museum is excellent, except that everything is only in Dutch, which I think is a mistake. There should at least be a translation into English. Also in the

Guide to the National Monument, also only in Dutch, there are
several stories of Jewish children and adults, most murdered in
one of the death camps or concentration camps. According to
the Museum, they "died" in those camps! The word *murdered* is
never used. This visit to Vught brought back to me terrible
memories of the horrors that took place there. For the survivors
of the Philips factory workers, some of whom were interviewed
for the documentary, Vught was just the beginning. They
received some extra rations from the other Philips workers, and
they were treated quite well at the factory. The real horror for
them came later upon arrival in Auschwitz and at the various
other camps where they were sent. I am one of the few children
of Vught to survive. Even if my story did not fit in with the
adults interviewed for the documentary, it should have been
part of it as the "memories of a child survivor."

Although there is a monument for these 1269 children, there
is none for the rest. Nearly all the children who were in Vught
were murdered in the death camps. The names of those children
should have been part of the children's memorial, maybe a
separate segment. The records are available at the Netherlands
Institute for War Documentation.

Photograph of part of the Monument to the children of Vught,
Netherlands, murdered in Sobibor June 11, 1943. Note names of Isaac
Menist and Jetty Menist. National Monument Camp, Vught, Netherlands.

Return to Dinslaken

I will not make their thoughts my own
by hating people for their race.
— "Race," Karen Gershon

I never had any desire to return to Dinslaken after the war. As a matter of fact I had decided never again to set foot on German soil. We were living in England and I remember my mother going to Holland in 1950 together with my sister to visit her stepmother, Sophie Berghausen, who had survived the war in hiding. My mother continued on to Dinslaken, which is fairly close to the Dutch border, to visit the Jewish cemetery and my father's grave. The cemetery had been terribly desecrated during *Kristallnacht* and totally neglected afterwards. She wanted at least to have her husband's grave cleaned up and the headstone restored. My sister decided to remain in Holland those few days and not to travel to Germany with my mother.

In 1951 I had decided to visit Holland, to visit my step grandmother and to see Amsterdam, Utrecht, and travel down to Maastricht, staying overnight at youth hostels with other young people. I did not want to go to Dinslaken, even though my mother would have liked me to check out the cemetery and my father's grave. I did go with some friends I had made in the youth hostels to Vaals, in the very south of Holland. This is the only hilly area in Holland and on top of a hill in Vaals, three countries — Holland, Belgium and Germany — meet. When we arrived on top of the hill, we saw some German police standing on their part of the border. We yelled insults at them and everybody joined in and called them *Moffen*, as we used to do when I was a child in Dinxperlo.

I did finally decide to return to Germany. What made me change my mind?

The year was 1989. I was by then living in the USA, was married, and had three children. I had been reading about Holocaust deniers, which upset me. I read about one particular professor from California, who claimed that he had visited Auschwitz, checked the so-called gas chambers but found no evidence of gas. He called the Holocaust a Jewish Zionist plot in order to garner sympathy from the world and collect reparations from Germany. Of course he never mentioned in his book that the Germans had blown up the gas chambers before they abandoned Auschwitz. It would be very difficult to find anything in the ruins of the gas chambers and crematorium after over forty years.

I felt that the time had come to talk to my children and tell them what had happened in those dark years. For them to understand better I decided the family should go on a trip to Europe, specifically to Holland and Germany, despite my vow never to set foot again in Germany. So in the summer of 1989 we left for Holland and Germany—my wife Yael, my son Omri, my daughter Avital, only 10 years old at the time, and I. My middle son Yuval who suffers from autism did not accompany us.

I had written to the *Burgermeister*, the mayor of Dinslaken, that we would be coming to Dinslaken, to visit my father's grave. I did not hear anything until a few days before our departure.

Then we received a telegram that we were invited to come to Dinslaken, that they had reserved a hotel for us, and that we should stay for at least two days. We stayed eight days in Holland, visiting Amsterdam, Enschede, Arnhem, Dinxperlo, and Gennep where we visited the grave of my grandfather, Louis Spiegel, in the tiny Jewish cemetery.

I did not really recognize Dinxperlo. The village had become bigger and seemed quite prosperous. The old post office had been rebuilt as a library. I was able to find out where our house had been. From the outside, it looked exactly the same. When I knocked on the door, nobody answered. Maybe there was nobody home, or whoever was in the house did not want to answer.

There is no barbed wire between Dinxperlo and Sudawick. The border street had different lamps on the German side, and the name was spelled slightly differently on the Dutch side. This was the only sign that you had crossed the border. This was not the Dinxperlo I had known; I knew nobody. No Jews were left in a village where once there had been a Jewish community with a synagogue. I felt like a stranger and did not stay very long.

I really did not know anybody there anymore. The few Jewish families who had survived were no longer living in Dinxperlo. Only recently did I establish contact with one of the people whom I had known well while I lived there—Willy Lieber, the son of the postmaster. He is retired and lives in the nearby city of Nijmegen. He actually found me because some articles I had written about happenings in Dinxperlo during the war had been translated into Dutch and German and posted on the website by Ferdinand van Loopik, a resident of Dinxperlo, who was the moving force for erecting the memorial to the Jewish community in Dinxperlo. I met Ferdinand on my second visit to Dinxperlo, in 1998. The purpose of that visit was to see the memorial and meet Ferdinand, who since has become a good friend.

We then went to Westerbork, the transit camp in Holland where I had stayed eight months in 1943 and also to Maastricht and Vaals.

I was very reluctant to continue to Germany and cross the border. However we were expected in Dinslaken, which was not too far away. Upon arrival at the hotel, they told us that we had been expected a day earlier. The receptionist called City Hall to announce our arrival. She told us that soon Mr. Jürgen Grafen would meet us. After a short time, Mr. Grafen arrived to welcome us. He gave us a book he had written, *Leben und Untergang der Synagogengemeinde Dinslaken, The Life and Destruction of the Jewish Community in Dinslaken*. They made us very welcome and showed us around everywhere. We went to the Jewish cemetery, which had been completely restored and was in immaculate condition. We found my father's grave and also the grave of my grandmother, Regina Spiegel, who died in 1919. After two days in Dinslaken we continued on to Hanover in order to visit Bergen-Belsen. There is not much to see there— only a museum, a memorial and mass graves of all those who had died in the last terrible months and who had been left lying all over camp. For the British had burned down the camp after liberation because of the typhus. We continued on to West Berlin. Germany then was still divided into East and West Germany and from Berlin we went to Nuremberg, Munich, and Frankfurt and back to Holland.

After this first visit, we became very friendly with Jürgen Grafen and his wife, Uschi. In November of 1993, Dinslaken decided to have a reunion of all surviving members of the Jewish community who had once lived in Dinslaken. The occasion was the 55th anniversary of *Kristallnacht,* November 9 and 10, 1938. A memorial to the thriving Jewish community that once existed was to be unveiled. People came from all over the world and I met people whose names I had known from my mother, but I had never met. We were really a small group, some people came with their children, but the event was well organized and I made many new friends and the people in Dinslaken we came in contact with were very nice.

By then I had started to lecture in schools and colleges about my experiences during the Holocaust. I found it much easier after I had been back to Holland and Germany and met some people there.

At the beginning of 2000 I received a letter from a teacher, Mrs. Gabriele Khanna. She told me that her high school, the *Theodor Heuss Gymnasium,* had a workshop and project about the Holocaust and the events of those years in Dinslaken and the fate of the Jewish community. They wanted to interview me because part of their project was to interview Holocaust survivors from Dinslaken. They had a partner city in Israel, Arad, and they would take the project there when the class visited Israel and Arad for *Yom HaShoah,* Holocaust Remembrance Day. I received several emails with a lot of questions from the twins, Brigitte and Christiane Steinhoff. I answered them and told them as much as possible. I had met them in Westerbork, and we had agreed to meet again that summer, when we were planning to pass through Dinslaken on our trip to Israel and Europe.

We have visited Dinslaken every year since 1998 because we became very friendly with the Grafens and are always very welcome there. We also met Edith Marx in Dinslaken, a Holocaust survivor who, when she became sick, moved back to Dinslaken after many years. Jurgen and Uschi Grafen took care of her as if she were their mother. The kids of the high school also interviewed her. Her mother, Jeanette Wolff, had been active in the Social Democratic Party in Dinslaken before Hitler. She was arrested in 1933, after the Nazis came to power because she was a Social Democrat. After surviving the horrors of several concentration camps, Jeanette Wolff decided to stay in Germany with her daughter. She was elected to the German *Bundestag,* or parliament, as a representative of the Social Democratic Party. She died in 1979.

Dinslaken Comes to the United States

Behold, God of Abraham, God of mercy,
Open your eyes as you have opened mine,
Open your eyes and see what I have seen.
 —"A Song Lost and Found Again," Elie Wiesel

In March of 2001, during spring break, I accompanied a group of undergraduates from The Richard Stockton College of New Jersey, to Holland and Germany. We visited Westerbork, and the next day on the way to Maastricht I persuaded Professor Hayse, who had planned the trip, to travel via Dinslaken and stay there for a few hours. I advised the city that we were coming. Upon arrival the *Burgermeisterin*, the mayor of the town, met us for a reception. Then we were shown around the town, passing by the memorial, to a church where the high school had its exhibit, as it was Ecumenical week. We were met there by the students; Gabriele Khanna, their teacher; and Professor Klaus Tofahrn, who worked with them.

The staff from Stockton College—Michael Hayse, Leo Lieberman, Gail Rosenthal, and Maryann McLoughlin—was impressed with what they saw and also by the students' knowledge of the English language. Then we discussed the possibility of bringing a small group of students to Stockton College to show their exhibit at the college and to local schools. After our return from that trip, we started to organize the visit of the Dinslaken students. As Stockton College could host them only for one week, I decided to approach Brookdale Community College in New Jersey, where I was also active, whether they could also host the kids for one week. Through the efforts of Dale Daniels, the Brookdale Holocaust Center Director, and Professors Jane Denny, Sy Siegler and Jack Needle things were organized so that the kids could come to Brookdale also.

Everything was set and arranged and six kids came with their teacher Gabriele Khanna and Professor Klaus Tofahrn. They came despite the terrible events of September 11, 2001. They arrived on September 30, less than three weeks after that terrible event. Their stay here was very successful both at Stockton College and Brookdale Community College. I enjoyed being with them and participating in their program. Some of the kids were very young, only 15 years old. The oldest was 18 years. At the farewell party at Professor Michael Hayse's house, I told the two girls, Lisa Tekolf and Yvonne Kaiser, that I was adopting them as my "step granddaughters." They liked that idea very much and I am still in touch with them and see them when I visit Dinslaken.

In the spring of 2002, six kids were invited to Nova Scotia through arrangements made by Professor Dorota Glowacka whom I had met at a conference. I flew to Halifax to be with them for a few days. Three of the kids had been in New Jersey in September/October 2001, one of those was Lisa Tekolf and three were new. Their teacher and professor accompanied them again. Their presentations were well received and I again actively participated. The kids were happy I was there, especially Lisa. I stayed with my good friend Professor Martin Rumscheidt and we had some nice parties at his house. Despite his wife Barbara's terminal illness, they enjoyed our being there.

A third group of six kids came in the beginning of April 2003, invited by Professor Bjorn Krondorfer of the St. Mary's college in Maryland. Because he could only host them for a few days, I tried to find something in Washington, DC, for them through the good offices of my friend Betsy (Elisabeth) Anthony, who works in Survivor Affairs at the United States Holocaust Memorial Museum. She made some very good contacts, but it still was not enough.

Then at the suggestion of Jürgen Grafen I contacted Marsha Pinson who lives in Washington, DC. Marsha is the daughter of Dorothy Stiefel, originally from Dinslaken, where her name was Thea Eichengrun. I had met them when Marsha came with her mother to the reunion in Dinslaken in 1993. I was somewhat hesitant to call Marsha because she was going through a difficult time: her husband had suddenly passed away about one year earlier. However, I did call her and she was very pleased that I had and she was ready to take care of everything. Her youngest son Max's *Bar Mitzvah* was to be held a week after I had phoned, but she assured me that everything would be done after that.

A completely new group of kids arrived in Washington, DC, on April 5, 2003. Again Gabriele Khanna and Professor Tofahrn accompanied them. Betsy and Marsha went to meet them at the airport; Marsha had rented a van especially to transport them during their stay in Washington. I arrived in Washington on April 6 and joined them the next day. The kids were all very young but did a great job. After spending the week with them in Washington, I got to know them very well. Talking to them at length I came to the conclusion that they were actually already the fourth generation. Their grandparents are younger than I am which means that at the end of World War II they were eight or nine years old, not old enough to understand. I asked a group of survivors at the Holocaust Museum in Washington, "How can I blame the third or fourth generation for what happened during those terrible years?"

Nowadays I speak a lot at schools about my experiences. I

am very often asked, "Did you ever return to Germany? And what is your attitude towards the Germans?" I always tell them, I cannot blame today's generation for what their grandparents may have done. I also believe you have to forgive, but never forget.

Those who cannot remember the past are condemned to repeat it.
—George Santayana

September 11, 2001

Clouds pass over, endless
Black fruit dripping
Sap from the branches
Of lightning.
   —"Passover: The Injections," William Heyen

One of the most deadly and destructive terrorist attacks happened on September 11, 2001 in New York and Washington, D.C. Nearly 3000 innocent people were killed. The twin towers of the World Trade Center collapsed and some adjacent buildings were completely destroyed. In Washington part of the Pentagon was destroyed. In western Pennsylvania, despite resistance, airline passengers, crew, and terrorists perished

When I speak in schools about my experiences during the Holocaust, the children many times ask, "What is your reaction to what happened? And "What were or are your feelings?" This is not an easy question to answer. How do you explain that there are people who are willing to crash airplanes into buildings and die in order to further their cause, intelligent people, but religious fanatics who had been planning this for a number of years? Suicide pilots and bombers are unfortunately nothing new. The Japanese in the Pacific in World War II had their *kamikaze* pilots who were willing to crash their airplanes into American ships. In Israel suicide bombers are almost an every day occurrence. And American embassies abroad and American military installations have felt the wrath of suicide bombers. However, nobody expected this on American soil. This has changed our lives forever.

When I first heard the news and saw on television what was happening, it seemed unbelievable to me. I was not frightened so much as I was angry. Thousands of innocent lives were lost because of religious fanaticism, because of extremism by people who want to rule the world, as the Nazis did, and put the world back into the Middle Ages, killing anybody who stands in their way, even if it means mass suicide.

There is some connection between September 11 and the Holocaust.   The Nazi Party was a terrorist party.   They systematically assassinated leaders of parties opposed to their policies. They sent the S.A., a para-military organization, into the streets to terrorize the population. When they came to power, they held on to it by terror, killing their opponents or putting them into concentration camps. They even killed many of the people who had helped them get to power, for example the bloodbath of "The Night of the Long Knives" in 1934.

For children the Holocaust is ancient history. It happened many years ago in the time of their grandparents. For them what happened on September 11 must have been a tremendous shock, especially for those directly affected by what happened. How do we explain to them that there is so much hate in this world? For all of us September 11 was a rude awakening to reality. We have to teach the children that the future is theirs to create.   First, we must work to stop this madness of racism, bigotry and antisemitism, so that the Holocaust and disasters like the terrorist attacks on September 11 will never happen again.   Then when we defeat our common enemies: terrorism, racism, and fanaticism, we can face the future with confidence.

CHAPTER THIRTY-FIVE: REFLECTION

Postscript

After the end of the world
after death
I found myself in the midst of life
Creating myself
building life

—"In the Midst of Life," Tadeusz Rozewicz

The summer of July 2003, I traveled to Israel and Europe together with my wife Yael. As part of the trip, we went to a reunion in Dinxperlo, Holland, of several classes from the general or public school of the year 1942. This was organized mainly by Willy Lieber, the son of the postmaster of Dinxperlo in those days, and Henk Lammers, my neighbor, who had lived three houses down from my Uncle Max's house on the Polstraat.

About twenty-four people came to the reunion; of those about fourteen were people who lived in the village in those days. The twenty-four was many more than I had expected because most of them no longer live in Dinxperlo. The event took place at a local restaurant. I really did not remember any of the people, even though I recognized some of the names. There were two class photos of 1942, apparently of the fourth and fifth grade, taken in the beginning of that year because, a short while later, all Jewish kids were expelled from what was then called the general school. A Catholic and a Christian (Protestant) school were also in the village in those days. I am in the picture of the fourth grade, with the teacher Mr. Florijn, whom I actually remember well as he lived not too far from us. When I looked at both pictures, I did remember nearly all the Jewish kids because after we were expelled from the regular school, we traveled together every day for about nine months to the Jewish school, in nearby Doetinchem, about 25 km away, for all the Jewish kids living in the *Achterhoek*, as this part of Holland was called. Unfortunately most of these Jewish kids were later murdered; however, a few families did manage to go into hiding.

We had decided beforehand that the official language of the reunion would be German, which most people probably would understand better than English. I had invited children from the Theodor Heuss Gymnasium (high school) in Dinslaken, Germany, to attend the event; Dinslaken is only about an hour's drive from Dinxperlo. Four children came, Anne Schmitz, Alexander von Busch, and my adopted granddaughters Lisa Tekolf and Yvonne Kaiser. Gabriele Khanna, the teacher who organizes the Israel AG, and Jorg Heininger, another youth organizer, accompanied them. I was very pleased that they had come.

After short speeches by Willy Lieber and Ferdinand van Loopik, a resident of Dinxperlo and a friend, who had pressured the village to put up the memorial in 1995 with the names of the Jewish residents of Dinxperlo who were murdered during the Shoah, I was asked to say a few words. I thanked everybody for coming, after all those years, sixty-one to be exact. I told them I was pleased that they were interested enough to come and meet with me.

After that Henk Lammers stood up and said, "I just have one question: 'How did you manage to survive, while your cousin Alfred and his family were murdered?'" I explained to him in a few words why I had been sent to Bergen-Belsen and what had happened to me. He then gave me a brochure which he had prepared for the reunion, in which there was the copy of a letter, written by him on March 2, 2000 to The Dutch Institute for War Documentation in Amsterdam. He had remembered my Uncle Max's family who lived near them and that suddenly two young children, refugees from Germany, had joined them. He only remembered my first name Fritz; he was not sure whether our family name was Spiegel. He did not remember my sister's name. He was sure we had been murdered in Sobibor on July 2, 1943, together with the family Spiegel. He had wondered why neither my sister's nor my name appeared on the memorial, so he had checked the archives in Dinxperlo, but there was no record of us. He assumed because we were refugees that we had not been recorded there.

His question to the institute in Amsterdam was: "Was there any way to trace what happened to my sister and me?" He was sure that we were murdered with my uncle's family and that we would remain nameless: for him, a terrible thought. He hoped that the institute could give him some information. If not, he was sure that in the archives of the murderers there would be a record. The Dutch Institute replied on June 28, 2000, confirming that my Uncle Max, Aunt Paula, and Cousin Alfred had been murdered in Sobibor, but that my cousin Ruth had survived. Furthermore, they wrote that the two children, Fritz and Edith Spiegel, survived, having been liberated on a train near Farsleben, Germany, on April 13, 1945. They had no further record of what had happened to us afterwards. On July 7, 2000, a further letter from the Institute told Mr. Lammers that he should contact the United States Holocaust Memorial Museum in Washington, where they have records of nearly all survivors. I was rather surprised that, fifty-five years after the event, people were still interested and trying to find out what had happened to their neighbors.

We walked through the village to see the house where I had lived with Uncle Max and his family. We entered, but of course it looked different. We also saw the houses where some of the other Jewish families used to live. The Villa Pol no longer existed. The school no longer exists but we saw where it had been. We then walked to the memorial, which was very sad for me when I saw the names of so many of my childhood friends.

Then we walked back to the restaurant and had a cool drink, the afternoon was quite warm. Some of the people had already left and it was time to say goodbye to Gabriele and the Dinslaken children. I knew that I would not see them again soon. I feel very close to them because I had spent a lot of time with them when they came to the USA to present their project on the Holocaust. I feel especially close to Lisa, and we try to keep in touch and also with Yvonne. Anne and Alexander are really wonderful children as are all the children participating in the Holocaust project. They are third and fourth generation and they are building bridges into the future.

The reunion took place on July 26, 2003. Unfortunately Willy Lieber, who played such an important part in organizing the reunion, died suddenly just a few weeks after the event. His sudden death shocked me. I am grateful for the times we spent together, first in August of 2002, when I met him during our visit to Holland after so many years, and then again this year at the Dinxperlo reunion. I am grateful for all the wonderful times we spent with his wife, Henny, and him. May he rest in peace.

Overcoming the Childhood that Was Lost

Professor Dan Bar-On, Ben Gurion University of the Negev

I t is always fascinating that you can know a person on some superficial level for many years, as I knew Fred Spiegel; you can even know some details of his life story (that he was a child survivor, that he survived a childhood under Nazi occupation in Holland and a period in Bergen Belsen), but until you read his whole life-story, as described so eloquently in this book, you do not have a real picture, just bits and pieces.

This was also a common reaction of some of my students at Ben Gurion University, when they would come back from an interview with one of their parents who were Holocaust survivors. In many cases they had known bits and pieces of the stories before, but could not make a whole picture and therefore felt that they lived "in the silence" of that painful past.

One can of course claim that there are many layers to a life-story and that we will never be able to reconstruct all of them. Still, I feel that Fred Spiegel has succeeded in providing us not only with many remarkable details of his lost childhood but also with some of the more important feelings that accompanied his memories of those difficult days: for example, his fears during the aftermath of the *Kristallnacht* or in the Vught camp, his joy during the early period in Dinslaken (his memory of the park there, the one that now seems so "small"), his longing for his mother and the painfully short encounter before she left for England on September 1, 1939.

I would like to present here a more comprehensive approach that tries to integrate the historical facts, the psychological impact on the people involved, and the social context in which these facts were reconstructed and deconstructed over and over again. When we look at Fred Spiegel's story, there is a feeling that in spite of the very difficult events Fred had to go through as a little child, he maintained a positive feeling concerning himself and others around him. After many years, Fred even reconciled with the Germans, from some of whom he suffered so badly, even developing some new friendships in his original hometown. How can we account for that? How did he succeed in doing this while others did not?

Fred's story is presented in a certain social and historical context—a well to do assimilated Jewish family who lived in Germany for many generations and was well integrated there (including the participation of his forefathers in WWI), with branches of the family in other European countries, specifically Holland. The Nazis broke up the existing social context by setting up one fate and context for all Jews, regardless of their diverse social and cultural backgrounds, trying to annihilate their psychological and physical existence.

However, if one wants to understand how families and individuals, who came from such different social and historical backgrounds, coped with the external attack on their existence, the original separate characteristics should be taken into account. Fred Spiegel and his family were perhaps among the fortunate ones; they had an option about where to go as late even as 1939, settling down temporarily in Holland. In addition, Fred was privileged to be with a few of his close relatives most of the time in Holland and with his older sister, Edith, even in the more difficult stages of the camps in Holland and in Bergen Belsen. At a critical moment he and his sister were saved by his uncle's brilliant idea to put them on the list of British citizens in Westerbork. This finally helped bring them to Bergen Belsen instead of Sobibor or Auschwitz.

But still, we can feel the moments when everything seems to weigh him down, especially when he was already so weak and ill in Bergen Belsen, with all the corpses around him and with the hope for an end to the war dwindling further and further.... In the aftermath of the war and the Holocaust, how did he recover from these terrible moments?

Fred Spiegel was one of the privileged to arrive in Holland relatively safely after the war, and to be traced by his relatives and brought to his mother who had searched for him and his sister. What an extremely difficult encounter for two children to meet their mother, who lived in relative safety during the war, after they have been through hell. I have an uncle who has a similar story. He survived Bergen Belsen (his father did not) and arrived in England after the war, taken in by one of his cousins, until he recuperated and could continue to USA to meet his mother who arrived there shortly before the war. I know how difficult his encounter with his mother was, when they reunited in Seattle after the war, and lived there relatively close to each other until she died recently.

Bert Lang, in his excellent article in Jewish Social Studies (1996)[12] asked two simple questions: Why did we, the Jews, not take revenge on the Germans after the war and why are we not interested in this question? In comparison to the fantasies of the camp prisoners during the war, acts of violent revenge were few and relatively short lived. Six million people were murdered, hundreds of thousands survived: Why did so few take revenge? On some level, I believe it has to do with the wanting to be able to look in the mirror again. Revenge can kill you morally and emotionally, just as it can kill your opponent, and the surviving Jews wanted to live as human beings, to be able to look in the mirror again, at least at some point in their future.

For many survivors there was one deep wish after the war: I don't want Hitler to win the war against us. The question was— What did it mean not to let him win? One answer was to rebuild life, to marry, have children, find a new country to live in safely, go back to work. This practical approach definitely meant that Hitler did not win the war against the Jews, as he wanted to stop such continuation of physical Jewish life. As important as this type of triumph was, it did not cover all realms and meaning of life.

I feel that Fred Spiegel's life-story represents this unbelievable ability of child survivors as human beings to sustain their humanity under those extreme conditions and to follow that line later in their lives. The small details of his life story tell us what it meant to go through all that and yet to remain not only alive, a survivor, but also a human being, showing his love to his fellow people and developing the ability to transmit that radiation of love to the following generations.

ENDNOTES

---

[1] Metzer, Milton. "Why Remember?"

[2] My grandfather had been a widower since 1919, when his wife, my grandmother Regina, had died during the flu epidemic of 1918-19.

[3] The Jewish School had been established in the early 1900s around the same time as the Jewish Orphanage. Before the Nazi regime not every Jewish child went to a Jewish school.

[4] On October 28, 1938, Germany expelled Jews with Polish citizenship, including the Abosch family, to the Polish border, where 17,000 Jews were stranded in the frontier town Zbaszyn, Poland.

[5] Britain cancelled all visas issued to people with German nationality, or who were living in enemy territory after the declaration of war on September 3, 1939.

[6] Westerbork was established by order of the Dutch government on October 9, 1939, as the *Centraal Vluchtelingen-Kamp Westerbork* (General Refugee Camp Westerbork). The Jews themselves paid for this camp.

[7] At his trial, Gemmeker claimed that he did not know about the gas chambers. This was of course absurd because he was a high-ranking officer in the SS who went to Berlin frequently for consultations on how to transport the Jews from Holland to the gas chambers as smoothly and quickly as possible.

8 The writer, Clara Asscher Pinkhof, was part of this transport. She later wrote a book, _Starrekinder_ (*Children of the Stars*), about her experiences.

9 Albala was tried *in absentia* in Athens, Greece, as a German collaborator. He was sentenced to death; however, the sentence was never carried out. Albala disappeared somewhere.

10 In April 1945, Josef Holstein, who had been evacuated earlier, was liberated by Russian troops on a train near the town of Trobitz, across the Elbe. I found out later that his parents and all his siblings, except for one younger sister, died. However, Josef, despite everything, always remained very religious. Many of that group who faithfully prayed every day did not survive, but those who did became very often even more religious. I did not.

11 *Kibbutz Yad Mordechai* is named after Mordechai Anielewitz, the leader of the Warsaw Ghetto Uprising of Passover Eve, April 19, 1943 to May 16, 1943. Anielewitz was killed on May 6, 1943, in the Command Bunker on *Mila* 18.

12 Lang, B. (1996). "Holocaust memory and revenge: The presence of the past." *Jewish Social Studies*, 2, 2, 1-20.

13 All the maps, except the one of the concentration camps in Part III, came from the website www.cia.gov/factbook. The map of the concentration camps came from www.ushmm.org.

14 The epigraphs for the Parts and the Chapters, for the most part, came from *Holocaust Poetry*, Hilda Schiff, ed. (New York: St Martin's P, 1995) and *Art from the Ashes*, Lawrence Langer, ed. (New York: Oxford UP, 1995).

About the Author

Fred (Fritz) Spiegel was born in Dinslaken, Germany, in 1932, the second child of Sigmund and Elise Spiegel. His sister Edith is four years older. Fred's family had lived in that part of Germany, the Rhineland, for many generations. His father served in the German army in World War I, as did all his uncles. His family was religious but much assimilated. They considered themselves Germans of the Jewish faith, no different from any other German.

In December 1933, when Fred was just one year old, his father died, so he really does not remember him. His earliest memories are of being called "dirty Jew" while playing with neighborhood kids in the park behind his house. Because some of the bigger kids assaulted him, Fred's grandfather decided to take him to play at the Jewish Orphanage, as it was much safer there.

Fred vividly remembers *Kristallnacht* the night of broken glass, November 9 and 10, 1938. The synagogue in Dinslaken was burnt. Jewish homes were smashed, windows were broken and everything was thrown onto the pavement.

Fred together with his sister was sent to Gennep, Holland, to live with an uncle. His mother managed to get a visa as an "au pair" maid to England and left on the last passenger ship from Holland to England on the first of September 1939, the day the German army attacked Poland.

On May 10, 1940, the German army invaded Holland. Fred and his sister left Gennep and moved to Dinxperlo, Holland, to live with a different uncle. From there in April 1943, together with his sister, he was taken to Vught, a concentration camp in the south of Holland.   After six weeks in Vught, he was transported to Westerbork where he remained for eight months, before being deported to the so-called "exchange camp" Bergen-Belsen in January 1944. In the beginning of April 1945, Fred and his sister were put on a cattle train and taken eastwards. The train was stopped by American troops near Magdeburg on the River Elbe on April 13, 1945. This was liberation.

Fred returned to Holland in May 1945 and went together with his sister to live with his only surviving uncle.   In November 1945, they went to England to be reunited with their mother whom they had not seen for six years.

In November 1952, Fred immigrated to Israel, where he remained for six years, living on a *kibbutz* and serving in the army. In December 1958, Fred went to Chile to visit his mother and sister, who had immigrated there some years earlier. Fred arrived in the United States of America from Chile at the end of 1963. He worked for four years for ZIM Lines, before joining EL AL Israel Airlines as their sales manager in New Jersey. After almost thirty-two years in EL AL, he retired at the end of 1998. He spends a lot of time lecturing at schools and colleges about his experiences as a child during the Holocaust. He is also associated, part time, with Gate 1, a tour operator of Glenside, Pennsylvania, selling groups and travel abroad. Fred is married to Yael, a Sabra (Israeli), and has three children

CHRONOLOGY OF EVENTS

Apr. 21	**1932**	**Fritz (Fred) Spiegel is born in Dinslaken, Germany.**
Jan. 30	1933	Adolf Hitler became Chancellor of Germany.
Dec. 4	**1933**	**Sigmund Spiegel, Fritz's father, dies.**
Sept-Dec.	1935	Enactment of Nuremberg Laws rendering Jews stateless.
Mar. 12	1938	Anschluss or annexation of Austria.
Nov. 9-10	1938	Kristallnacht (Crystal Night or Night of Broken Glass).
Nov.	**1938**	**After *Kristallnacht* (Crystal Night) Fritz and sister Edith leave for Holland to live with Uncle Adolf and Aunt Martha in Gennep.**
May 17	1939	The British Government issues a "White Paper" effectively stopping Jewish immigration to Palestine.
Sept. 1	1939	German forces invade Poland.
Sept. 1	**1939**	**Fritz's mother Elise travels on an *au pair* visa via Gennep to England on the last passenger ship to leave.**
Sept. 3	1939	Great Britain and France declare war on Germany
May 10	1940	German forces invade Holland.
May 13	1940	Dutch Government and Royal Family flee to England.
May 15	1940	Dutch armed forces capitulate.
June 6	**1940**	**Grandfather Louis Spiegel dies in Gennep.**
June 25	**1940**	**Fritz and his sister Edith move to Dinxperlo to live with Uncle Max and Aunt Paula.**
July 14	**1940**	**Alice Spiegel, cousin of Fritz and daughter of Adolf and Marta, dies; she was just 11 years old.**
Oct. 5	1940	Non-Jewish government employees must sign a declaration of Aryan purity.
Nov. 21	1940	Jews are fired from all government positions.
Jan. 10	1941	Mandatory for Jews to register with the Town Registrar.
Feb. 5	1941	Members of the medical profession must sign a declaration of Aryan purity.
Feb.13	1941	The Nazis form a Judenrat (Jewish Council) for the city of Amsterdam.
Feb. 22-3	1941	Razzias (raids) for Jews carried out in Amsterdam.
Mar. 31	1941	Nazi operated German central office for Jewish emigration is established in Amsterdam.
May 1	1941	Jews must surrender all radios.
June 22	1941	Operation Barbarossa begins; Germany invades the Soviet Union.
Aug. 8	1941	Restrictions imposed on the Jews' financial and property matters.
Sept. 15	1941	Signs reading "Forbidden for Jews" appear in all public places.
Oct. 7-8	1941	Razzias for Jews held in many cities in Holland.
Nov. 7	**1941**	**Jews must obtain a permit to travel or move.**
Dec. 11	1941	Germany and Italy declare war on the United States.

Jan. 9	1942	Jewish children are expelled from all public schools.
Jan. 9	**1942**	**Because he is Jewish, Fritz has to leave local public school and go to a Jewish school in nearby Doetinchem.**
Jan. 20	1942	The Wannsee Conference of top Nazi leaders is held in Berlin suburb of Wannsee. The "Final Solution" to the Jewish question.
Jan. 23	1942	Identity cards must show the letter J.
Mar. 25	1942	Jews forbidden to marry non-Jews.
Apr. 24	1942	Ritual slaughtering is forbidden.
May 3	1942	Jews ordered to wear the yellow Star of David with Jood inscription.
May 12	1942	Jews are forbidden to own a state bank account. Monies are confiscated.
June 5	1942	Jews may not buy in non-Jewish stores.
June 12	1942	Jews may no longer play sports. They must turn in bicycles and cars.
June 30	1942	Nazis introduce an 8 PM curfew; order all Jews off the street at night.
July 1	1942	The Nazis take over the Centraal Vluchtelingenkamp Westerbork (Central Refugee Camp Westerbork), which becomes the Judendurchgangslager Westerbork (Jewish Transit Westerbork).
July 15	1942	Deportation from Westerbork to the "Resettlement or Work Camps" in Poland begins.
Aug.	1942	Jews in Holland subjected to Razzias (raids) almost nightly.
Aug.-Dec.	1942	Weekly deportations from Westerbork, east to Auschwitz, continue.
Jan.-Dec.	1943	Weekly deportations from Westerbork, east to Auschwitz, continue, including nineteen trains to the death camp Sobibor starting March 2 1943 through July 20, 1943.
Jan.16	1943	The first Jews arrive in Concentration Camp Vught from the prison at Amersfoort.
Jan. 21	1943	Patients of the Jewish Mental Hospital in Apeldoorn deported directly to Auschwitz.
Apr.	1943	Jews living in the southern provinces of Holland must report to camp Vught.
Apr. 10	**1943**	**Fritz, Edith, and family of Max Spiegel sent to Concentration Camp Vught in the south of Holland.**
May 23	**1943**	**Fritz and family transported to Transit Camp Westerbork.**
May 25	**1943**	**Fritz is taken off transport whose destination was Sobibor, Poland.**
May 26	1943	Intensive Razzias for the remaining Jews of Amsterdam and other large cities.
June 6-7	1943	Two transports from Vught take the remaining children, 1269, to Westerbork. The following day they are transported to Sobibor and murdered upon arrival.

June 29	1943	Uncle Max, Aunt Paula, and cousin Alfred transported east to Sobibor, where they are murdered on July 2. **Fritz and Edith enter orphanage in Westerbork.**
Nov.16	1943	Most of the children in the orphanage are transported to Auschwitz where they are murdered. Fritz and Edith are among the children to remain behind.
Jan. 11	1944	First deportation from Westerbork to "Exchange Camp" Bergen-Belsen.
Jan. 11	1944	**Fritz and his sister are put on transport to so called "Exchange Camp" Bergen-Belsen.**
Sept. 3	1944	Last deportation train from Westerbork to Auschwitz, which includes Anne Frank and her family
Sept. 13	1944	Final deportation train from Westerbork to Bergen-Belsen
Sept.	1944	Concentration Camp Vught is abandoned by SS.
Jan. 27	1945	Soviet troops liberate Auschwitz.
Apr. 12	1945	Liberation of Transit Camp Westerbork by Canadians— only about 800 Jews were still in the camp of a total of about 105,000 who passed "through" Transit Camp Westerbork.
Apr. 7	1945	**Fritz and Edith are put on transport from Bergen-Belsen eastwards.**
Apr. 13	1945	**Fritz's train liberated by American troops near Magdeburg on the river Elbe.**
Apr. 15	1945	Liberation of Bergen-Belsen by British troops.
May	1945	**Fritz and his sister are transported back to Holland. They are taken off the train in Maastricht, Holland, and put in separate hospitals. Fritz was suffering from typhus and malnutrition.**
May 7	1945	Germany signs an unconditional surrender at U.S. General Dwight D. Eisenhower's headquarters at Rheims, France.
July	1945	**Fritz and his sister are sent to the Jewish Orphanage at Laren near Amsterdam. Uncle Adolf finds them there three days later.**
July-Nov.	1945	**Fritz lives with his Uncle Adolf and Aunt Marta in Utrecht, Holland.**
Nov.	1945	**Fritz, now Fred, and Edith are reunited with their mother in England after six years' separation.**

KEY:
Bold=Fred's Chronology